JENNY HASKINS
PRESENTS A

# galleria
## OF MACHINE ARTISTRY
## AND QUILTING

A Galleria of twenty-nine amazing machine
artists and quilters, along with the directions to
make the *Black & White Dreams* quilt.

Brewer
*Quilting & Sewing Supplies*

To order this book – Brewers Quilting and Sewing Supplies
Phone Toll Free: 1800 676 6543
Email: info@brewersewing.com

First published in the USA in 2009
Brewers Quilting and Sewing Supplies

Author: Jenny Haskins
Assistant: Simon Haskins
Designer: Jo Martin
Subeditor: Nina Paine
Graphics: Simon Haskins
Photographer: Tom Evangelidis
Styling: Robyn Wilson and Jenny Haskins
Publishing coordinator: Simon Blackall

National Library of Congress
Cataloguing-in-Publication Data applied for
Haskins, Jenny
Haskins, Simon
A Galleria of Machine Artistry and Quilting

ISBN 978-0-9841582-0-1

Printed in China

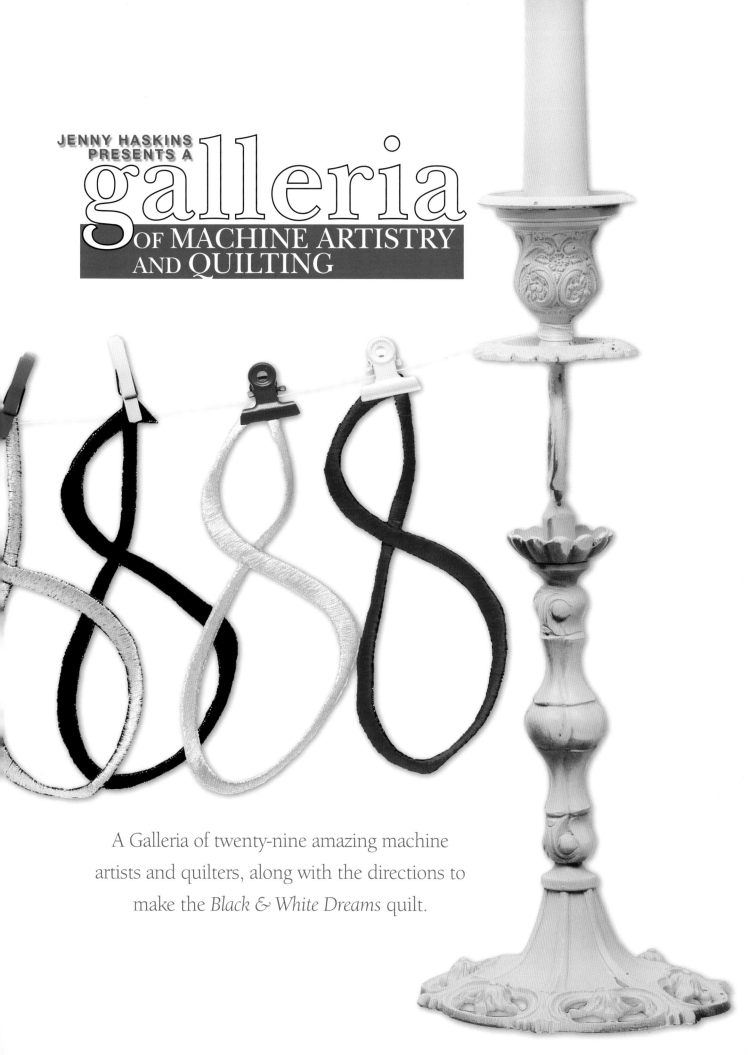

# JENNY HASKINS
## PRESENTS A
# galleria
## OF MACHINE ARTISTRY
## AND QUILTING

A Galleria of twenty-nine amazing machine
artists and quilters, along with the directions to
make the *Black & White Dreams* quilt.

Sewing and stitching are almost universal among human populations and date back to Paleolithic times (30,000 BC); in fact sewing predates the weaving of cloth. History attributes the invention of the earliest sewing machine to the Industrial Revolution, with the first working sewing machine invented by the Englishman Thomas Saint in 1790. The sewing machine fast became the prized possession of nearly every home, justified as a necessary cost-saving commodity (much like the family car of today), as it was used for the construction of family garments, household linens, and interior decorating items.

QUILTING IS PART of Australian history, with sailors on the tall ships that made their way to Australia (sailors who were also trained in the art of sewing as they had to mend the ships' sails) piecing quilts to pass the time during the six-month journey from England to Australia. For this they used discarded shirts. Early Australian settlers also made waggas, which were quilts made from discarded suiting and heavier fabrics (these were no longer of any use in the hot Australian climate). In many cases these waggas used old newspapers as batting, and the three quilt layers were held together with knotted string.

*A Galleria of Machine Artistry and Quilting* celebrates not only the launch of the *8-Series* Bernina machines, but the exceptional Australian artisans whose passion is machine artistry, embroidery, and quilting, and it is with much national pride and anticipation that Simon and I present, in this book, some of the most creative, dedicated, and honored machine artists and quilters that Australia has to offer today.

Simon and I were proud to be asked to write and publish this book, a book that would never have come to fruition had it not been for the support and vision of two amazing women and one man – Kerrie Hay and Greg Alexander of Bernina Australia, and Barbara Sunderlage of Brewers Quilting and Sewing USA. It was Kerrie's concept for the *Bernina Australasian Creative Challenge* – a concept that was eagerly supported by Greg and enthusiastically taken up by the Australian 'Friends of Bernina', whose work is showcased in this book. When I mentioned to Barbara that it was possible these amazing artworks would then be published in a book,

she immediately replied: 'When will it be out? Here is our order!'

Robbie (who is away on another cruise, would you believe), Simon, and I all took great delight in unpacking, ironing, and photographing these sensational garments, quilts, and hanging pieces, produced by the crème de la crème of Australian quilters, fiber artists, and art-to-wear artisans. Each piece in this collection is of museum standard and has been created by award-winning machine artists and quilters.

In one way or another (often through publications), Simon, Robbie and I have long been associated with sewing machines of all brands, and it has always been our mission to help spread and support machine artistry and quilting in its many forms. The joy that we receive from all who are involved (mostly women, but we don't want to leave the men out – Simon wouldn't appreciate that at all) when they have completed a work of art would be reward enough, but it's also amazing to see their confidence grow, not only in their chosen art form but in the way it can change their lives.

I remember when I first joined the sewing industry and made my first quilt. Never having made a quilt and knowing nothing about it, exact piecing was not high on my priority list; however, upon discovering that this was a prerequisite, and coming from a fine arts background, I simply sculpted three-dimensional flowers to place strategically over any of my less-than-perfect piecing! No-one knew and the quilt went on to be published. Following on from this was *The Heritage* quilt, one of the first (if not the first) machine embroidered quilts in Australia. Then came the *Color Purple* quilt, which was my first

internationally recognized quilt and today, over a decade later, is one that continues to be made. Simon and I have now lost count of the number of quilts we have designed and made, however the thrill we feel on completion of a quilt remains as strong now as it ever did!

Like Greg (see page 9), I can vividly recall the story of one of my very early customers. It was the last day at the *'Stitches and Craft Show'*. I was tired and waiting for the show to end when I overheard two ladies talking. 'It just isn't fair, it really isn't', one of them said. I was sure I was about to hear a complaint, so I was now listening with even greater attention and preparing my reply when they continued. 'How can these sewing machine companies expect us not to purchase their machines with the amazing samples they have on display!' I was pleasantly surprised and, true to their word, the ladies (a mother and daughter) each bought a machine.

At about the same time I was complimented by a USA-based president of one of the sewing machine companies on a garment I had on display. I explained that I had a great machine to work with, and he responded by saying that it was the driver behind the machine that made the difference. I believe it is a melding of both worlds, with the top-of-the-range sewing machines today being technical wonders of the twenty-first century – driven by extraordinarily gifted, talented, and passionate textile artists who can proudly hold their heads up high in the presence of any artist working in any medium in the world today. *A Galleria of Machine Artistry and Quilting* honors and showcases works of art from twenty-nine of these Grand Prix winning machine drivers.

So sit back, relax (with a glass of wine or a cup of tea), and indulge your creative senses as you venture into the world of machine artistry and quilting, and enjoy a private viewing of the work of these artists. You may also be inspired to make a piece of your own, with the directions for the *Black & White Dreams* quilt.

Remember that when you love yourself enough, you will make yourself a quilt or a piece of machine embroidered art.

*Jenny*

# contents

### EDITOR'S NOTE

Kerrie's picture defies the fact that she has been in the sewing industry for over 24 years. She lives in Sydney and is mum to two handsome young boys (Daniel and Cameron). Kerrie is the National Sewing Promoter for Bernina Australia and creator of the Latte Quilt and its accompanying book. I am proud to say that Kerrie is also a personal friend of Simon's, Robbie's, and mine. Although for years we worked for companies that were in opposition, we both respected each other's talent and expertise and soon became great friends – both of us had (and continue to have) the goal of promoting the world of machine artistry and quilting and keeping it inspired.

The *Bernina Australasian Creative Challenge* was Kerrie's concept and it was she who was the driving force behind it – the collection in this book is a testament to the admiration and respect the Friends of Bernina, along with the sewing industry in general in Australia, have for her. This book is a result of her passion (as well as Simon's and mine) – the type of passion Greg speaks about on page 9 – and we trust that passion will transfer from these pages to our readers.

AT BERNINA, it is our goal to generate and encourage a love of sewing to those who have a passion to create any form of art, be it craft, fashion, quilting, or embroidery. In doing this I am privileged to cross paths, form friendships, and learn from the many passionate men and women who come from all walks of life, and who choose to use the sewing machine as their chosen tool to produce world-class works of art.

When the word was out that Bernina was going to launch the Bernina *8-Series*, their latest top-of-the-range machine (I think it's their best ever), the challenge for me was to come up with a piece of work that depicted the capabilities of these new Bernina machines, from the simple elegance of a basic machine to that of a state-of-the-art one. How can you depict it all in just one piece of work, and by whom would it be made?

Over the years Bernina has been privileged to be associated with many leading artists who have come together to form an elite group we call the Friends of Bernina. This group is made up of artists from all over Australia who have chosen Bernina machines as their tools of trade, and have put their tools to the test as they strive for perfection and creativity at the highest level.

So, what better group to ask to participate in a challenge to create not just one but many wonderful pieces to showcase Bernina and what we stand for. The challenge was created with the *8-Series* in mind, so the colors black, red, white, and silver were selected to be used with a red number 8 (naturally!), in any way, shape, or form. This allowed for the creativity of each individual artist to be expressed in any way they so desired.

Bernina Australia put up a prize of a Bernina *830* machine and embroidery unit for the winning entry, and that entry would be kept by Bernina as a perpetual icon for the launch of the *8-Series* machines. All entries would then be displayed at the *8-Series* launches to be held in every Australian state. These works would also be exhibited at all the major shows for the following year.

The response to the challenge was overwhelming and beyond all my expectations. Upon viewing these works of art, I realized that they should not be limited to Australia, but should be proudly shown to the world, and what better way to do this than in a book.

I trust you will be as inspired and motivated as I have been as you view these amazing machine artists' works. Jenny has included contact details for each artist, so please email them and let them know how exciting and wonderful you think their work is, as we know they would love to hear from you, as would I. Let me assure you that if you are ever in Australia (or traveling near a location in which any of these tutors are giving classes), they are not to be missed.

I would like to leave you with this quote that expresses our thanks to each and every one of our Bernina Friends (including those who were not able to participate in the challenge):

*Friendship is a work of art, and should always be displayed in the best light possible.*

I trust we are doing just that in *A Galleria of Machine Artistry and Quilting.*

Kerrie

**You can contact Kerrie via email (Kerrie@bernina.com.au).**

kerrie hay

IT IS MY GREAT PLEASURE, on behalf of Bernina Australia, to contribute to the opening pages of *A Galleria of Machine Artistry and Quilting*, and I count myself as privileged to be able to invite you to enter a world of creativity and distinction in machine artistry and quilting.

I am into my ninth year in the sewing machine industry and, during this time, have learned a great deal about what makes this industry unique in so many ways.

Like most industries, the success of the sewing industry depends largely on profitability, product excellence, and exceptional service. Business is business when it comes to operating a successful organization, but that is where the similarity ceases. My passion is business, but I would like to share with you how that passion became even more pronounced.

I was six months into my role at Bernina when our office received a call from an irate customer. Being a new recruit and as a last resort (no-one else had been able to help this particular lady), it was my task to deal with her or with any distressed customer – irate or otherwise.

Prior to answering the call I was informed that the caller was a ninety-two-year-old woman who was more than a little upset! Upon answering the call I explained, in my most calm and professional manner, that I was here to assist and make sure, as a valued customer, we solved her problem. She informed me very quickly that her name was Beryl, and she went on to explain in no uncertain terms how she could not believe that at Bernina's head office we could not supply her with a spare part for her beloved Bernina sewing machine.

Beryl continued (very verbally) to explain that for a company such as Bernina not to be able to assist her was utterly ridiculous and that we should

do whatever was required to resolve her dilemma. Only then did I discover that the machine in question was in fact over forty years old! Upon enquiry as to why Beryl believed that the parts should still be available on such an antiquated machine, she simply replied that her 'baby' was still as good as new and had been running perfectly until this problem occurred. The thought of losing her 'baby' was heartbreaking to this lady, and certainly not acceptable.

I went on to explain that it would be unrealistic for sewing machine companies to stock parts on products indefinitely, and I gently suggested (being a salesman at heart) that she consider 'trading-up' to a new model Bernina, which as we all know has so much more to offer. Beryl then told me what she thought of my suggestion – it was as if I had suggested that she abandon her child.

I thought that my response to her tirade was sympathetic and valid and when I suggested that, with due respect, we were not talking about something as vital as a heart-lung machine, there followed a stony silence. After thirty seconds (which felt more like thirty minutes) she simply replied with the following statement: 'No sonny! It's far more important than that!'

I was completely taken aback and, not knowing how I should respond, I started laughing. Thankfully Beryl joined me and we continued chatting for some time – in the end Beryl purchased a brand new Bernina. At last report, both 'mother Beryl' and her 'new baby' Bernina were doing well, and I appreciate the valuable lesson Beryl taught me: it was about loyalty and passion for a product, and an industry that, in my experience, is not matched anywhere.

To this day I am grateful for Beryl's call and I would like to thank her for providing me with my first real taste

of the passion involved in the sewing industry, as well as the dedication and loyalty of its dealers, artists, and consumers. Following my 'Beryl' experience and in the ensuing years, I too acquired the same passion for the sewing industry, and the product and artistry that is Bernina.

Numbers at the end of the day are how we keep going, but it is not all about the bottom line. When I see the fulfillment and delight a sewing machine can bring to customers, I realize that there is so much more to life than profit.

As a fellow machine artist, would-be artist, or simply someone who is in awe of machine artistry and quilting, I know you are in for an awesome experience as you turn the pages of *Galleria*. You will be privileged to gaze upon some of the finest textile art, machine embroidery, and quilting works created by some of Australia's top sewing artists, and I know their enthusiasm for what they do will transcend these pages and you too will feel their passion.

I am proud to have contributed to this publication and I would like to thank Jenny Haskins for her amazing editing and for publishing this book, which in itself is a work of art.

I would also like to thank our wonderful Australian 'Friends of Bernina' who gladly took up the challenge and allowed us to publish their fine artworks. I extend full credit to Kerrie Hay for the initial concept of the *Bernina Australasian Creative Challenge* to launch the *8-Series* machines that in turn instigated the whole process – thank you Kerrie, you are simply the best!

I would like to leave you with the concept of keeping the passion going as we venture into the future of the *8-Series* machines.

Greg

greg alexander

What is it that is so exceptional and different about the Bernina name in Australia, and in particular the new *8-Series* machines? What inspires such loyalty to a brand and such response from artists for the launch of a new machine?

What sets the Bernina *8-Series* apart from any other top-of-the-range machines? Having briefly sewn on one of these new machines in Houston, my first impression was that a woman must have had a big say in the design of its features – and sure enough she had! It has constantly amazed me that an industry comprised predominantly of women has always been managed by men, and simply driven by the passion of the women who keep it going. But finally a company has got it right!

And it's not just me who thinks so. We put the question – 'Why the *8-Series* machines?' – to the public, and here are the reasons (in no particular order) they came up with.

■ I have amazing speed with control sewing with or without the foot control – like cruise control on a car.

■ The easily accessible bobbin as it 'pops' out when the bobbin door is opened makes it so easy for less than perfectly active hands.

■ The jumbo bobbin – lasts longer giving me more time to be creative and less time in preparation.

■ The 30 LCD 'runway lights' are fabulous. I no longer need additional lighting day or night no matter what color my fabric is.

■ Fluid light, smooth, and fast – runs like a Ferrari – should be red!

■ Compact built-in dual feed lets me say goodbye to pins – perfect piecing no matter what the fabric is.

MAYBE IT'S THE SUPPORT that this company gives to the art of sewing, its contributions to machine artistry and quilting guilds, exhibitions, and individual artists. Maybe it's the education and training it so freely supplies to both dealers and consumers. And maybe it's their willingness to supply machines to tutors for classes, or to deliver a machine to a hostel when an artist has a deadline to meet and she is with her sick daughter in hospital.

Perhaps it is the Managing Director, the Sewing Promoter, the Education Consultants, or the service, the warehouse, or the spare parts department. Or maybe it's the fact that it is a family owned and operated company. Most likely it's a combination of all these attributes. When you read what the 'Friends of Bernina' say in the following pages you will realize that all of the above are contributing factors to what makes Bernina so exceptional. But the thing that shines through most is the passion and dedication these machine artists have to an art and their tools – the Bernina machines.

As a consumer, all this would definitely influence me in the decision as to what machine to purchase, but why this machine in particular?

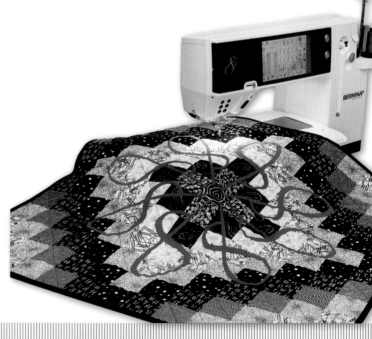

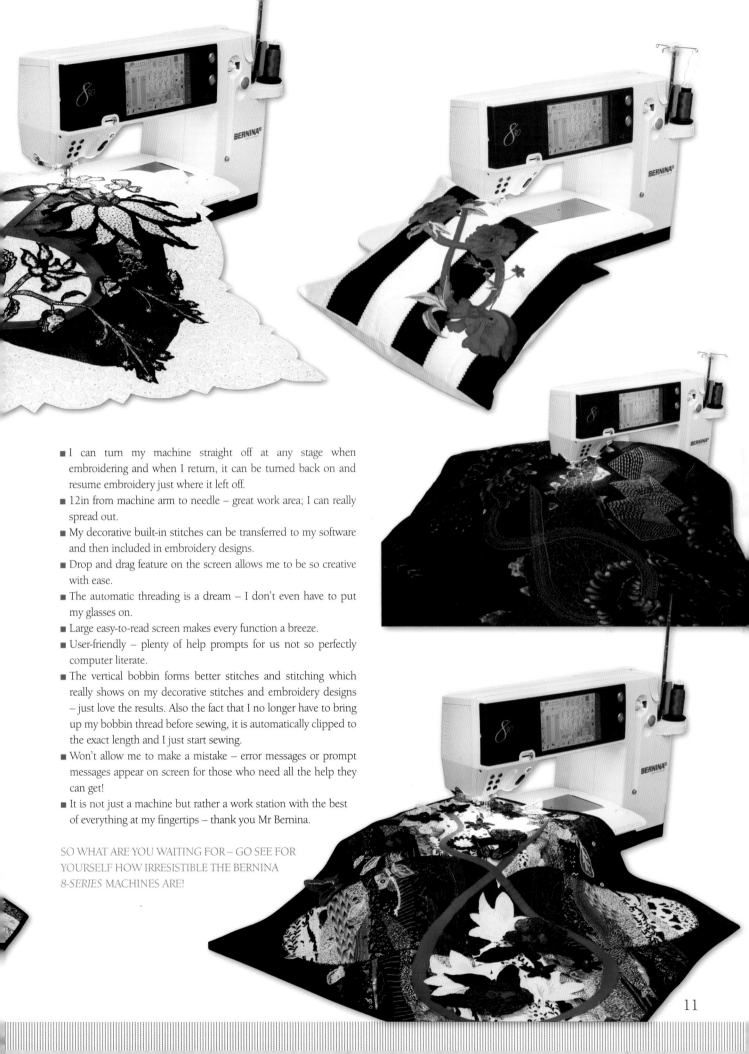

- I can turn my machine straight off at any stage when embroidering and when I return, it can be turned back on and resume embroidery just where it left off.
- 12in from machine arm to needle – great work area; I can really spread out.
- My decorative built-in stitches can be transferred to my software and then included in embroidery designs.
- Drop and drag feature on the screen allows me to be so creative with ease.
- The automatic threading is a dream – I don't even have to put my glasses on.
- Large easy-to-read screen makes every function a breeze.
- User-friendly – plenty of help prompts for us not so perfectly computer literate.
- The vertical bobbin forms better stitches and stitching which really shows on my decorative stitches and embroidery designs – just love the results. Also the fact that I no longer have to bring up my bobbin thread before sewing, it is automatically clipped to the exact length and I just start sewing.
- Won't allow me to make a mistake – error messages or prompt messages appear on screen for those who need all the help they can get!
- It is not just a machine but rather a work station with the best of everything at my fingertips – thank you Mr Bernina.

SO WHAT ARE YOU WAITING FOR – GO SEE FOR YOURSELF HOW IRRESISTIBLE THE BERNINA 8-SERIES MACHINES ARE!

KIM BRADLEY
GLENHAVEN, NSW, AUSTRALIA

Kim has now been quilting professionally for seven years and loves every minute of it. She started back in the early 1980s, making quilts for her children (rather badly she confesses), but then had a long break as she focused on the sewing that needed to be done for five boys, rather than her own passion of quilting.

IT WAS NOT UNTIL MUCH LATER, when Kim moved to Australia from New Zealand, that her infatuation with quilting returned. She was amazed at how the industry had grown, in both popularity and style. All this had passed her by, but she was inspired rather than deterred by the prospect of 'catching up' with the quilting world.

Quilting is Kim's way of expressing herself, and she loves the opportunity to dream up new quilting patterns, always pushing the boundaries with the prospect of innovative designs that express who she is.

Kim met Jenny (Haskins) in 2006 – a most fortunate meeting as it turns out because she asked Jenny to look at her work, seeking advice as to what color fabric to bind a quilt she had just finished. With Jenny's encouragement and insistence, Kim entered her quilt in the IQA Market and Festival, which is held annually in Houston, and to her joy and excitement it was accepted!

Jenny, who is a great friend and admirer of Kerrie Hay, recommended Kim to Kerrie. As a result (and much to Kim's delight), she was invited to become a 'Friend of Bernina'. This was a great validation for Kim – working on a Bernina machine was easy for her as her mother and sister had both been sewing on Bernina machines for years.

Soon Kim was making regular appearances at all the major quilt and craft shows across Australia and New Zealand, demonstrating on the Bernina stand and teaching quilting and embroidery classes on their machines.

Kim takes pride in the fact that in 2006 she introduced Australia and New Zealand to her 'Kwilt Kolor Koncept', which uses Derwent *Inktense* pencils to shade and color her lavish feather-quilting designs. This technique has taken the quilting world by storm as it enhances, emphasizes, and adds definition to quilting. As a result of this, the Cumberland Pencil Co in England used one of Kim's quilts in their worldwide advertising, and also commissioned her to create a quilt for their company.

Kim has taught her 'Kwilt Kolor Koncept' extensively in both Australia and New Zealand and, as a result, color enhancement of quilting using this concept has now become extremely popular, especially with the young, attracting a whole new generation of quilters.

Kim has received awards at such prestigious quilt shows as the 'Australian Quilt and Craft Fairs' held across Australia and New Zealand. She has won the 'Australian Machine Quilters' Conference' Rookie Award, First Prize at the 'Victorian Quilt Show', and numerous viewers' choice awards from local quilt shows. She also does commission quilts for corporate and private collectors around the world.

In 2008 Kim was asked to be the guest tutor, judge, and keynote speaker for the biannual New Zealand Longarm Quilting Symposium, and then in 2009 she was privileged to teach at the 'Australasian Quilt Show' in Melbourne.

As an innovative quilter, Kim has been featured in all the major Australian quilt and embroidery magazines: *Creative Expressions*, *Down Under Quilts*, *Australian Patchwork & Quilting*, *Country Threads*, *Patchwork & Stitching*, *Homespun*, and *Quilters Companion*. Her work has also featured in *The Australian Women's Weekly* magazine, and in two books: *Material Obsession* and *Fandango*.

Kim's quilting patterns, which she sells under the name of Kim Bradley Creations, have been used by quilters who have won major prizes at quilt shows both nationally and internationally – a great thrill for winners and Kim alike. She also produces embroidery patterns for domestic machine embroidery, and now produces her own kits, using hand-dyed fabrics along with color enhancement techniques, for commercial sale. More recently Kim has added a novelty fabric print to her ever-growing stable of products, all of which can be viewed on her website.

Kim's quilting career is just beginning, and what a beginning it is as she learns to spread her new wings, inhaling the rarefied atmosphere that only eagles breathe. We cannot wait to see where this flight takes her.

**You can contact Kim via email (kim@kimbradleycreations.com), or visit her website (www.kimbradleycreations.com) to view her quilts, products, and teaching schedule.**

# BERNINA AND ME
## *Kim Bradley*

Winner of the *Bernina Australasian Creative Challenge* for the launch of the
Bernina *8-Series* machines

Kim considers it an overwhelming honor to win the *Bernina Australasian Creative Challenge*. Late in 2008, after thinking about it for some time, Kim drew up her quilt design on paper to get a feel for how she wanted to portray what Bernina meant to her. She wanted her quilt to represent how she is drawn to and split between contemporary and traditional quilting designs, and how the two can be linked.

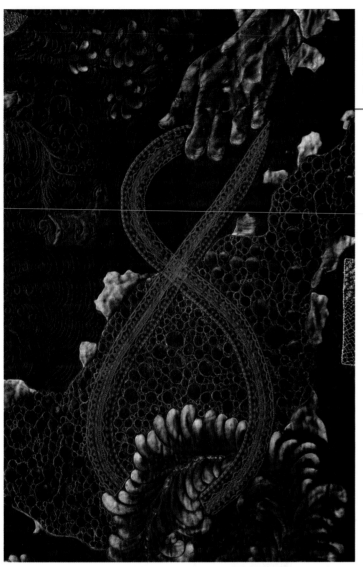

The red '8' in the center represents Kim's interpretation of the release of the new machine range, with Bernina' turning a fresh page. The edges of the quilt are turned in like a folded page with the '8' pushing the pages out in the center, as if the edges of the page are torn back through the center of the quilt.

The '8' is stitched using the built-in decorative stitches on Kim's Bernina, as are the small set of blocks to the right with the stitches going in different directions and lines, creating shades of light through to dark. These blocks represent the challenge for every Bernina owner – with so many decorative stitches built into the machine the sky is the limit, and a machine artist is only limited by her imagination.

The top half of the quilt is quilted with myriad intricate contemporary quilting designs representing the way quilting is evolving. The *BSR* makes it possible for all quilters to achieve perfect quilting, even on a domestic sewing machine.

The quilting styles then move through one another and flow – almost like one design is inspiring the next to be created.

The hand (which is modeled from Kim's own hand) is stitched as if it were pushing through the page and grabbing the '8' for inspiration, giving anyone the ability to turn dreams into reality.

The elaborate quilted feathers at the bottom of the quilt snake through the base of the '8' and pull it down; this shows Kim's desire to remain true to traditional quilting styles and the fact that she is torn between the two.

In the top right corner of the quilt, near the turned-back page and on the edge of the fabric, is a stitched eye, looking to the future and wondering what Bernina will think of next. Kim cannot wait!

# Black & White Dreams

Lizzy Allen

Lizzy (with a little help from her son Josh) chose to craft a virtual 'scrap' quilt to celebrate the launch of the Bernina 830. Using patchwork piecing embellished with glorious machine embroidery, *Black & White Dreams* is finished off with Lizzy's stunning custom quilting.

LIZZY ALLEN
HEATHCOTE, VIC., AUSTRALIA

Patchwork and quilting have always been Lizzy's first love; while she enjoys and admires other crafts, it's always a quilt she just has to make next.

Lizzy had been sewing bridal gowns for many years when she was at a craft show and saw her first longarm quilting machine. That was it – she knew she had to have one. It was ten years ago when she purchased a Gammill longarm quilting machine, and now she can't imagine doing anything else but quilting.

LIZZY DISCOVERED SHE COULD 'DRAW' with a needle and thread, as every new quilt was a blank canvas that she could admire and enhance. She started a small business in country Victoria where she was living, and is honored to have quilted many quilts that have been featured on the front covers of numerous quilting magazines and books. Lizzy's quilting journey has been simply incredible.

Delighting in custom quilting, Lizzy soon had a thriving custom-quilting business called *Thimble and Thread*, which kept her much-loved Gammill working almost twenty-four hours a day. It wasn't long though before her small studio needed to be enlarged to accommodate her machines and fabric stash. Being in the middle of the terrible 'black Saturday' bushfires, Lizzy, her family, and their home escaped harm, but they knew then that living on tank water was too much for them, and so they decided to move. They now have town water, and the bliss of having a shower that lasts more than a minute is heaven! Just as blissful is that with a new home came a larger studio for Lizzy!

As Lizzy truly believes that only God is perfect, she would like to pass on to would-be-quilters her philosophy on quilting: As much as we try to achieve perfection, we should remember to enjoy what we are making rather than achieve perfection, which is not a state but rather a journey! Remember to have faith in yourselves, as nothing in quilting is ever a mistake, it is rather just your unique creative interpretation. Not all quilts we make are supposed to be award-winning, yet when we give one as a gift, suddenly it becomes perfect in the eyes of the receiver and after all, that is what counts.

Machine embroidery is Lizzy's passion – a girl cannot have too many threads nor too many embroidery designs (and of course there are never enough hours in the day to finish that last design). She loves the idea that we can truly design our own patterns and choose our own colors and style with each quilt block we create, using a different technique or style; she loves that we can make laces, trims, three-dimensional flowers, and embellish a quilt to our heart's desire.

Lizzy achieved First Place in the 'Premier Festival of Machine Embroidery Quilts' in July 2007 (sponsored by the magazine *Creative Expressions*), winning the wonderful Bernina Artista 640 embroidery machine. It has been one of the most memorable events of Lizzy's career.

A chance meeting three years ago saw Lizzy being asked to work with the Floriani and Jenny Haskins' products team based in the US and headed up in Australia by Hans Martini; she was very excited about this opportunity. Ricky and Kay Brooks taught her a great deal about their products and presentation skills, which opened another door on her machine embroidery journey. Now currently working for Know How Sewing Essentials Australia, teaching, and demonstrating at all major quilt and craft shows around Australia, Lizzy was further honored with the opportunity to attend the Jenny Haskins' Academy of Accredited Tutors, and in September 2008 became an accredited Jenny Haskins' teacher. This has proven to be another highlight of Lizzy's career, enabling her to travel around Australia, meet fabulously talented people, and teach Jenny Haskins' classes. Working with Simon and Jenny is a dream come true for Lizzy, and one of the best parts of her ongoing career, as working with Jenny is inspirational.

**You can contact Lizzy via email (lizzy@thimbleandthread.com.au), or visit her website (www.thimbleandthread.com.au) for more information on her custom quilting, teaching, and schedule of appearances.**

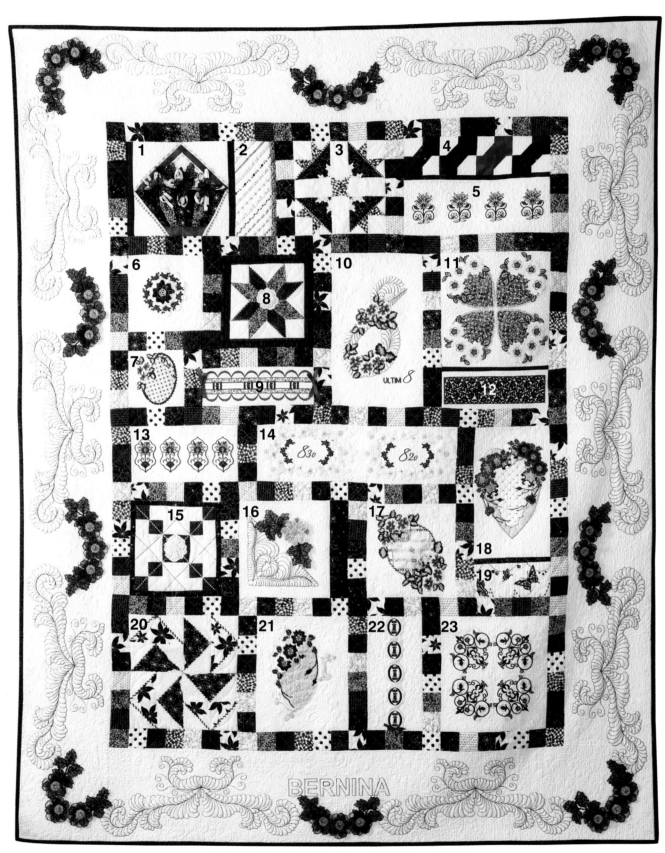

FINISHED SIZE OF QUILT – 69in x 85in (175cm x 216cm)

*Black & White Dreams* evolved when Lizzy was asked (as a 'Bernina Friend') to enter the *Bernina Australasian Creative Challenge* to launch the *8-Series* machines, and thus have a chance of winning a Bernina 830 (every girl's dream machine).

With no boundaries on creativity other than the specified and limited color palette of black, white, red, and silver, Lizzy knew there was a quilt 'in-the-waiting'. The challenge was to determine what direction the quilt would take; however there was no question at all that machine embroidery would be a big part of it – machine embroidery is Lizzy's obsession.

With her two children on school vacation at the time, and frustrated with the familiar phrase, 'Mum, I'm bored' at a time when she was busy trying to finish quilting a client's quilt, Lizzy was desperate to occupy them. She decided she would show them how to sew a foundation-pieced patchwork block. The basket block is from one of Jenny Haskins' cushion designs (one of her licensing classes). It is full of beautifully embroidered three-dimensional flowers. Joshua loved the idea of the foundation piecing and Meaghan wanted to make the embroidered flowers – an hour later they reappeared, presenting Lizzy with a black and white basket with a red handle; the next step was the embroidered flowers and, once it was completed, the block was stunning.

This wonderful little basket of flowers suddenly became Lizzy's inspiration for a sampler quilt, one that could be achieved by anyone – after all, if her children could make a block, anyone could. It was also a wonderful way of using all the features on her Bernina 640 sewing and embroidery machine. With so many fantastic designs by Jenny and Simon Haskins, the fun really began. Coupled with Jenny's *Perfect Quilt* software, Lizzy started to design her *Black & White Dreams* quilt. She wanted the quilting designs to stand out and had decided that some of them would be stitched in black thread – Kim Bradley's quilting designs where just perfect for this. And so the quilt grew, block by block. She was thrilled with the end result and trusts that anyone who makes *Black & White Dreams* will enjoy it every bit as much as she did.

# MATERIALS

NOTE: As this is a scrap quilt, fabric quantities will vary depending on how they are to be used and cut.

- Bernina *8 Series 830/820* embroidery/sewing machine and accessories
- Bernina embroidery software *V5/6* and transfer device
- Bernina large oval *Jumbo Hoop*: 260mm x 400mm (smaller hoops, for example the *Mega Hoop*, may be used but this will require multi-hooping)
- *Galleria* design CD (included FREE with this book)
- *1,200 Classic Foundations* and *Easy Strip Piecing* Perfect Quilt software for patchwork pieced blocks
- Fabrics:
  – 5yd x 45in (4.6m x 114cm) white tone-on-tone cotton fabric for blocks and borders
  – 18 fat quarters of black and white patterned fabric for pieced sashing, borders, and patchwork
  – one fat quarter each of red, gray with silver fleck, plain black, plain white, and black and white patterned cotton fabric for piecing and appliqué inserts
  – five fat quarters, one each of different black and white patterned fabrics for patchwork piecing
  – 81in x 97in (206cm x 246cm) backing fabric (allowing 6in (15cm) on each side for longarm quilting)
  – 1¹/₈yd x 45in (1m x 114cm) black fabric for binding
- 1yd x 45in (1m x 114cm) each of black, red, and white nylon crystal organza for Jenny's *Embroidered Decoupage* technique
- 2yd x ¹/₄in (2m x 6mm) each of red and white satin ribbon
- 1yd x ¹/₈in (1m x 3mm) black satin ribbon
- 5yd x 60in (4.6m x 152cm) bolt of *Quilt Magic* lightweight fusible batting (optional)
- 70in x 86in (177cm x 218cm) *Matilda's Own* cotton batting (optional)

- 6yd x 45in (5.5m x 114cm) *Sheer Magic Plus* to stabilize the white tone-on-tone fabric, piecing, and appliqué fabric
- *Hoop Magic* self-adhesive tear-away stabilizer for embroidery
- *Dissolve Magic* fiber-based soluble stabilizer
- *Template Magic* printable sheets to print embroidery designs
- *Tearaway Magic* printable sheets to print foundation-piecing templates
- *Appliqué Magic* pressure-sensitive double-sided fusible web
- Jenny's rayon embroidery threads: White No 98, Black SB, Metallic Silver G27, Merlot No 7, Cherry Divine No 675
- *Invisa* sheer thread
- Construction thread for needle and bobbin
- Fine black and white bobbin thread for embroidery bobbins
- White quilting thread for needle and bobbin
- Machine feet: embroidery No 26, ¹/₄in patchwork No 37, open-toe freehand No 24, open-toe No 20
- Machine needles: Bernina Embroidery 80/90, Metafil 90
- Heat-activated crystals (clear and ruby) and heating wand
- Jenny's *Magic Heat-Cutting Tool* for embroidered decoupage
- Glass or ceramic tile to use with heat-cutting tool
- Rotary cutter, self-healing cutting mat, quilting ruler
- Small sharp scissors
- Paper scissors
- Spray bottle and clean water
- Cotton/Q-tips
- Water-soluble fabric-marking pen
- Glass-headed pins
- Hand-sewing needle
- Compass
- Tracing paper and lead pencil
- Bodkin to thread ribbon through buttonholes
- General sewing supplies

## PREPARATION

*Black & White Dreams* is a scrap quilt, so when you are cutting your quilt sections to piecing size you will find your measurements differ to those given in these directions. You can either add another strip of fabric to make up the difference or cut a piece down – this quilt allows for plenty of flexibility with the fabric measurements.

That said, every effort has been made to provide all the measurements for fabric cutting and piecing as accurately as possible, and although quilt measurements vary from person to person, depending on how the fabric is cut and pieced, it will help you to try to follow theses directions as closely as possible. Techniques such as embroidery, appliqué, and quilting can alter the size and shape of a fabric piece, so please check your measurements against the ones given below and then adjust yours if necessary. Remember you can always add one or two strips of fabric to a block to ensure it is the size used in the quilt.

## FABRIC

NOTE: All fabric will be cut using a rotary cutter, self-healing cutting mat and quilting ruler on a need-to-use basis. The embroidered quilt blocks and borders will be first cut larger than needed and then cut to piecing size once the embroidery is completed.

1 Use a hot steam iron to press 5yd x 45in *Sheer Magic Plus* (wrinkle-free) to the back of the 5yd x 45in white tone-on-tone fabric. By doing this you are adding a thread count to the fabric as well as stability to prevent the fabric puckering as it is embroidered. (You may choose to do this to all your fabrics as the *Sheer Magic Plus* strengthens the fabric, makes it easier to cut and piece, and prevents it from fraying.)

## EMBROIDERY

NOTE: The embroidery designs used in *Black & White Dreams* have either been combined or enlarged to take advantage of the Bernina Jumbo Hoop area to minimize fabric hooping. If you have a hoop that is smaller than 260mm x 400mm you will have to modify the designs to fit your hoop area and then multi-hoop your fabric to achieve the same design effect.

2 The embroidery designs used in *Black & White Dreams* are taken from:
– Josh Allen's *Feather Quilting '8'* design – p.allen30@bigpond.com (Josh is Lizzy's son)
– Bernina *Artistic Adornments* design CD – www.bernina.com.au
– Kim Bradley's *Feather Quilting* design CD – www.kimbradleycreations.com
– Jenny Haskins' design CDs: *Beyond Color Purple, Gracious Impressions, Rosebuds, Lace Glorious Lace, Designer Neckties, Victorian Roses* – www.jennyhaskins.com

NOTE: All the embroidery designs needed to make the *Black & White Dreams* quilt (excluding lettering fonts) are included on the *Galleria* design CD that comes free with this book; we thank the designers for generously giving us permission to copy and then give these designs free for a one-time-only use in this book.

## MARKING EMBROIDERY BLOCKS

3 Use the fabric-marking pen and quilting ruler to mark all blocks that are to be embroidered directly onto with vertical, horizontal, and diagonal lines that intersect at the center of the fabric.

## EMBROIDERY

4 All embroidery uses the following: the large oval *Jumbo Hoop* (260mm x 400mm) for optimum ease of embroidery, or the *Mega Hoop* (which will require multi-hooping or resizing of some designs); the *Embroidery 80/90* needle for rayon thread and the *Metafil 90* needle for metallic thread; machine bobbins wound with fine black and white bobbin thread; Jenny's rayon and metallic embroidery threads; an embroidery foot; and either *Hoop Magic* self-adhesive tear-away stabilizer or *Dissolve Magic* fiber-based soluble stabilizer, hooped.

Clip all jump threads and remove or wash the excess stabilizer from the embroidery. Also remove any fabric-marking pen lines before pressing each block or embroidery piece from the back over a towel.

5 Use the Bernina *V5/6* software, the free *Galleria* design CD and the transfer device to transfer the designs to the machine on a need-to-use basis.

## SELF-ADHESIVE TEAR-AWAY STABILIZER

NOTE: Always use your basting stitch option when using this technique – this secures the fabric to the stabilizer around the outside edge of the design area and ensures your fabric doesn't move.

This stabilizer is used in quilt blocks 5, 6, 7, 9, 10, 11, 12, 13, 14, 16, 17, 18, 21, 22, and 23.

6 *Hoop Magic* self-adhesive tear-away stabilizer is used for designs that are embroidered directly onto fabric, and it comes in 10yd rolls, in two widths (12in and 20in) to accommodate your hoop size. This stabilizer is used for most embroidery designs that would normally require fabric hooping. *Hoop Magic* doesn't remove the pile from fabrics (especially batting) and it is eco-friendly, tearing away easily from the back of the embroidery. Should the item be washed, the stabilizer disintegrates into the water leaving the embroidery free of stabilizer.

– Use paper scissors to cut a piece of self-adhesive tear-away stabilizer to suit your hoop size. It should be approximately 1 1/2in wider and longer than the hoop you are using. Hoop the stabilizer as you would fabric, with the protective coating uppermost in the hoop.

JENNY'S TIP: Cut a good supply of stabilizer to hoop size and keep it close by, rather than cutting a piece each time you need it. Purchasing a second

hoop for your machine is a good idea – that way you can have the next hoop ready to go once you have completed your embroidery.

- Use a pin or sharp object to score diagonal lines (piercing the protective coating only) that intersect at the center of the stabilizer in the hoop, as well as around the inside of the hoop. Next, use a pin to lift each of the four sections of protective coating from the center (these should come off easily with the help of the score lines).
- Call the selected design up onto the machine screen. Make sure it is in the center of the screen and that the needle is in the center of the design.
- Place the hoop in the machine and then place the fabric to be embroidered over the sticky stabilizer in the hoop, so that the intersecting placement lines match those marked on the hoop and the needle sits at the point where the two lines intersect. Also make sure that the mark you made on the fabric for the top of the hoop matches the top of the actual hoop once the fabric is placed on the stabilizer.
- The idea of using sticky stabilizer in the hoop is so that you can move the fabric on the stabilizer rather than the design on the screen. It also saves re-hooping your fabric time and time again, and helps to achieve accurate placement with ease.

## PRINTABLE TEMPLATE SHEETS
**This technique is required should you not have a Bernina Jumbo Hoop.**

**7** Use the Bernina design software to separate, reduce or divide the embroidery designs found on the *Galleria* design CD so that they fit your hoop area. Next, save them under a new name. Use the design software to print these designs on *Template Magic* printable sheets (which are backed with reusable temporary adhesive) and then use the transfer device to send them to your machine. Print the required number of design templates for any one combination design (for example, if there are four designs in the combination, print four templates), and then use paper scissors to roughly cut around each design template.

- Use the block photo and the marked divide lines on the fabric (see step 3) to position these temporary adhesive design templates on the fabric, matching the positions of the designs on the block.
- Place the fabric on the hooped self-adhesive tear-away stabilizer and position it for the first design so that the divide lines on the template match the marked corresponding positions on the hoop.
- Select the first design on the machine screen so that it is centered in the hoop and the needle is centered in the design.
- Place the hoop in the machine and ensure that the needle is centered in the design – reposition the fabric if necessary.
- Remove the template (replacing the backing paper so it can be used again) and use the basting stitch to hold the fabric to the stabilizer and embroider the design.
- Repeat these steps as many times as it takes to replicate the block designs on *Black & White Dreams*.

## JENNY'S EMBROIDERED DECOUPAGE
### (Cut-and-paste embroidery)
**8** Loosely defined, embroidered decoupage is an embroidery design that is stitched out over hooped nylon organza and stabilizer. Several options can be used; we suggest the following. While the stabilizer and nylon organza are still hooped, place the hoop (right side up) over a glass or ceramic tile. Using the fine tip (the heat-cutting tool comes with several tips), trace around the embroidery outline. Follow the embroidery outline closely to remove the excess fabric from the edge of the design. Position this freestanding embroidery design on any fabric or garment, pin it in place and then, using *Invisa* sheer thread, sew a small freehand stipple-stitch around the outside edge of the design to adhere it to the fabric.

### Embroidered decoupage using soluble stabilizer
**This technique is used in quilt blocks 3, 8, 15, and 20.**

**9** Use a layer of white nylon organza hooped with *Dissolve Magic* fiber-based soluble stabilizer to embroider the lace designs used in these four blocks. Repeat the directions given in step 6.

### Three-dimensional embroidered decoupage
**This technique is used in quilt blocks 1, 14, 16, and the quilt borders.**

**10** Three-dimensional embroidered decoupage is when a design is stitched over the nylon organza hooped with *Dissolve Magic*, a fiber-based soluble stabilizer. If you need multiples of the one design, combine as many of the designs in one hooping as you can, color-sort them in your Bernina V5/6 design software, and then save the combination design. Then, while the fabric and stabilizer are still in the hoop, use the heat-cutting tool to heat-cut around each design as in step 6. Soak the freestanding designs in a tub of water, making sure you give them a final rinse in clean water to remove the stabilizer. Lay the designs flat over a towel to dry.

Great effects can be achieved by layering designs (such as flowers and leaves) with solid fabric designs. The base flower or leaf could be a solid color with sheer designs placed over the top so that the sheer petals sit between the solid ones rather than directly over the top of them. Combine these designs by stitching around the center of a flower or down the veins of a leaf.

These designs can now be used individually, grouped into a collage, or combined with other embroidered decoupage techniques.

### FOUNDATION PIECING
**This technique is used in quilt blocks 1, 3, 4, 8, 15, and 20.**

**11** Foundation piecing is achieved using a paper template with the patchwork design printed on it. The fabric is stitched in sequence over the marked lines to

create a patchwork design. The backing paper is removed once the piecing sequence is complete.

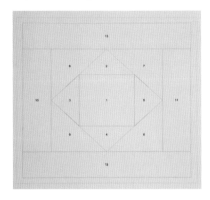

**12** Use *Tearaway Magic* printable sheets to print the foundation piecing templates:

From the *1,200 Classic Foundations* quilt software:
– Block 1: one 10in x 9in **Wicker Basket No 3**
– Block 4: four 4in square **Bowtie**
– Block 8: one 8in square **8 Pointed Star**
– Block 20: one 12in square **Dutchman's Puzzle**.

From the *Easy Strip Piecing* quilt software:
– Block 3: one 10in square **Cross and Crown**
– Block 15: one 9in square **Checkerboard No 2**.

**NOTE: If the block size you need is larger than the *Tearaway Magic* printable sheets, you may need to combine several sheets to make the template, holding them together with sticky tape.**

**JENNY'S TIP: You may find it easier to sew over the lines on the template with no thread in your machine, or use a tailor's tracing wheel to perforate the paper template over the guidelines. In doing this you can easily identify the**

lines from the back of the template, which helps when you are placing the fabric in the correct position for piecing.

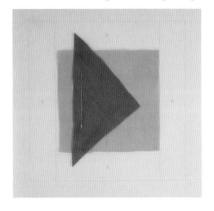

– Place the first piece of fabric over the template, wrong sides together. The second piece of fabric is then placed over the top of the first piece, right sides together. Sew along the first seamline.

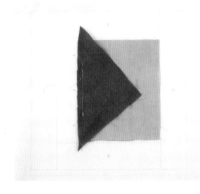

– Trim the seam back to $^1/_4$in.

– Flip the second seamed fabric back over the seam and press it.
– Continue in this manner until the template is covered with pieced fabric, following the number sequence on the template and pressing each additional fabric piece as you go.
– Press the completed template.

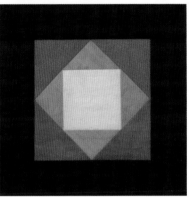

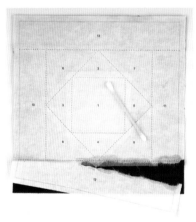

– Check that your fabrics are color-fast and then run along the marked lines on the back of the pieced template/block using a cotton-tip or Q-tip dipped in clean water. This softens the tear-away (which is eco-friendly, by the way) and makes it easier to gently tear the paper sections away from behind the pieced block.

You now have a perfectly pieced patchwork block ready to be included in your *Black & White Dreams* quilt. Should you find for any reason that the size of your pieced block is smaller than the one used in the quilt featured here, as this is a 'scrappy' quilt, simply add a strip of fabric to both sides or just one side of the block (as in block 1).

## WICKER BAKET NO 3

### TECHNIQUES:
FOUNDATION PIECING
DECORATIVE STITCHING
THREE-DIMENSIONAL
EMBROIDERED DECOUPAGE

BWD01

BWD02

**NOTE: Lizzy is a *Jenny Haskins' Accredited Tutor* and this block is one of the licensed classes.**

Refer to pages 21–23 for the *Foundation Piecing* and *Embroidered Decoupage* techniques.

### Foundation piecing
Use *Tearaway Magic* printable sheets to print the foundation template for a 10in square **Wicker Basket No 3** patchwork design from *1,200 Classic Foundations* Perfect Quilt software. Use the photo as a guide to the fabrics used to foundation-piece the square.

### Decorative stitching
Use black thread in the needle and bobbin with *Tearaway Magic* at the back of the stitching and an open-toe foot No 20 to sew decorative rows of stitching on the outside and inside edges of the basket and handle, and at the top of the red fabric at the bottom of the basket.

Stitches used:

Cut the block to a piecing size of 10$^{1}$/2in square and then join a 1in x 10$^{1}$/2in strip of black fabric to each side of the block.

Block 1 now measures 10$^{1}$/2in x 11$^{1}$/2in (piecing size).

### Three-dimensional embroidered decoupage
Hoop red nylon organza with *Dissolve Magic* and use red thread in the needle and bobbin for the flowers and black for the centers to embroider design **BWD01**. Re-hoop with black nylon organza and *Dissolve Magic* and use black thread in the needle and bobbin to embroider design **BWD02**.

Use the photo as a guide to layer the embroidered flowers and leaves over loops made from the 2yd x $^{1}$/4in white satin ribbon and the 1yd x $^{1}$/8in black satin ribbon, and then use the freehand foot No 24 and *Invisa* thread to freehand around the flower centers and along the leaf veins to secure them to the basket. Ruby crystals accent the flower centers.

## TECHNIQUE:
DECORATIVE STITCHING

Cut a 6in x 12in strip of white tone-on-tone fabric and then use the fabric-marking pen and quilting ruler to mark 3/4in spaced diagonal lines in one direction across the width of the fabric strip.

### Decorative stitching

Use the open-toe foot No 20, black thread in the needle and bobbin, and *Tearaway Magic* at the back of the fabric to sew rows of decorative stitching that are centered over the marked lines using stitches such as these:

There is no need to tie off at the beginning and end of each row of stitching as the fabric will be trimmed to piecing size after the stitching is complete.

This is such a fun way to play with the built-in decorative stitches on your *Bernina 8-Series* machine to create fabric.

Cut the diagonally decorative-stitched fabric to 5in x 10¹/2in, making sure that your rows of stitching are diagonally true. Cut a 1in x 10¹/2in strip of black and white patterned fabric and then join it to the right side of the decorative-stitched fabric, so that the rows of stitching go from right to left.

Block 2 now measures 5¹/2in x 10¹/2in (vertical piecing size).

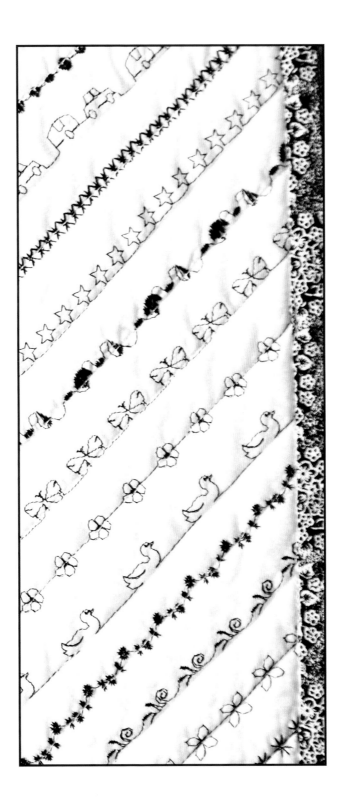

## CROSS AND CROWN

### TECHNIQUES:
FOUNDATION PIECING
DECORATIVE STITCHING
EMBROIDERED LACE
DECOUPAGE

Refer to pages 21–23 for the *Foundation Piecing* and *Embroidered Decoupage* techniques.

### Foundation piecing
Use *Tearaway Magic* printable sheets to print the foundation template for a 10in square **Cross and Crown** patchwork design from *Easy Strip Piecing* Perfect Quilt software. Use the photo as a guide to the fabrics used to foundation-piece the square.

### Decorative stitching
Use white thread in the needle and bobbin with *Tearaway Magic* at the back of the stitching and an open-toe foot No 20 to sew a row of decorative stitching centered over the seamline on the long side of the four center triangles.

Stitch used:

### Embroidered lace decoupage
Use white thread in the needle and bobbin. Hoop the white nylon organza with *Dissolve Magic* to stitch four

**BWD03** lace designs (these can be combined in one hoop area).

Use the photo as guide to place these four lace designs, evenly spaced around the center square, in the patchwork pieced block. Pin them in place and then use the open-toe freehand foot, with *Invisa* sheer thread in the needle, to attach the lace pieces to the block by stitching around the outside edge of each design.

Block No 3 now measures 10½in square (piecing size).

BWD03

## BOWTIE

### TECHNIQUE:
FOUNDATION PIECING

Refer to pages 21–23 for the *Foundation Piecing* technique.

### Foundation piecing

Use *Tearaway Magic* printable sheets to print four foundation templates for a 4in **Bowtie** patchwork design from *1,200 Classic Foundations* Perfect Quilt software. Use the photo as a guide to the fabrics used to foundation-piece the four squares.

Join the four designs horizontally using a $^1/_4$in patchwork foot. Use the photo as a guide to both the direction the bowties face and the fabric color sequence.

Block No 4 now measures $4^1/_2$in x $16^1/_2$in (piecing size).

BWD04

## TECHNIQUE:
EMBROIDER DIRECTLY ONTO FABRIC USING SELF-ADHESIVE TEAR-AWAY STABILIZER AND (OPTIONAL) PRINTABLE TEMPLATES

Refer to pages 21–23 for the *Hoop Magic* self-adhesive tear-away stabilizer technique for embroidering directly onto fabric, and (optional) the *Template Magic* printable sheets technique.

### Embroider directly onto fabric using *Hoop Magic* self-adhesive tear-away stabilizer

From the white tone-on-tone fabric, cut an 8in x 19in strip. Use the fabric-marking pen and ruler to mark vertical and horizontal lines that intersect at the center of the fabric. Use these marked lines with *Hoop Magic* self-adhesive tear-away stabilizer hooped to position the fabric over the stabilizer. Center and embroider design **BWD04** vertically on the fabric strip using the photo as a guide to the thread colors used.

### Optional – Template Magic printable sheets

If your hoop is not large enough to accommodate design **BWD04**, use the design software to split the design in half so that there are only two designs together. Save this new design and then send it to the machine. Print this design (twice) on *Template Magic* printable sheets and then use these templates to place the designs, evenly spaced and horizontally centered, on the fabric. From center to center of each design should measure 3³/4in; embroider the designs using the *Template Magic* placement technique so that they align vertically on the fabric.

Maintaining the embroidery placement (it should be centered horizontally in the fabric), cut the block to 6in x 16¹/2in.

From the plain black fabric, cut a 1in x 16¹/2in strip and then stitch this to the top of the block.

Block 5 now measures 6¹/2in x 16¹/2in (horizontal piecing size and maintaining the embroidery centered horizontally in the fabric).

**This block completes the first block row (Blocks 1 to 5).**

## TECHNIQUES:
EMBROIDER DIRECTLY ONTO
FABRIC USING SELF-ADHESIVE
TEAR-AWAY STABILIZER
EMBROIDERED APPLIQUÉ

Refer to pages 21–23 for the *Hoop Magic* self-adhesive tear-away stabilizer technique for embroidering directly onto fabric.

Embroider directly onto fabric using *Hoop Magic* self-adhesive tear-away stabilizer.

From the white tone-on-tone fabric, cut a 10in square. Use the fabric-marking pen and ruler to mark vertical and horizontal lines that intersect at the center of the fabric. Use these marked lines with *Hoop Magic* self-adhesive tear-away stabilizer,

BWD05

hooped, to position the fabric over the stabilizer. Center and embroider design **BWD05** on the fabric square using the photo as a guide to the thread colors used and black fabric as the appliqué insert.

### Embroidered appliqué
**NOTE:** *Sheer Magic Plus* **should be ironed to the back of the appliqué fabric as it not only adds stability to the fabric, it prevents it from fraying**

and therefore removes the possibility of the fabric pulling away from the outline stitching after the fabric is cut away. It also prevents the fabric from puckering due to the dense embroidery stitching.

Stitch the outline of the area in the design that has an appliqué fabric insert. Place the appliqué fabric centered over the outline stitching; the outline will be stitched again. Remove the hoop from the machine (not the fabric from the hoop) and then use small sharp scissors to carefully cut around the edge of the fabric, close to the row of stitching. Place the hoop back in the machine to complete the appliqué and embroidery design.

Block 6 now measures 8$\frac{1}{2}$in square (piecing size and maintaining the embroidery centered in the fabric).

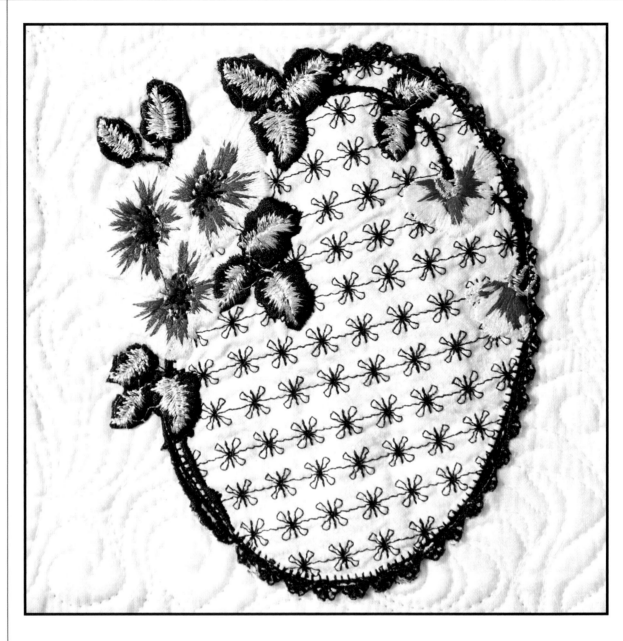

## TECHNIQUE:

EMBROIDER DIRECTLY ONTO FABRIC USING SELF-ADHESIVE TEAR-AWAY STABILIZER

BWD06

Refer to pages 21–23 for the *Hoop Magic* self-adhesive tear-away stabilizer technique for embroidering directly onto fabric.

### Embroider directly onto fabric using *Hoop Magic* self-adhesive tear-away stabilizer

From the white tone-on-tone fabric, cut an 8¹/2in square. Use the fabric-marking pen and ruler to mark vertical and horizontal lines that intersect at the center of the fabric. Use these marked lines with *Hoop Magic* self-adhesive tear-away stabilizer, hooped, to position the fabric over the stabilizer. Center and embroider design **BWD06** on the fabric square using the photo as a guide to the thread colors used. Omit the fabric appliqué option in the center of the oval.

Block 7 now measures 6¹/2in square (piecing size and maintaining the embroidery centered vertically in the fabric).

## 8 POINTED STAR

### TECHNIQUES:
FOUNDATION PIECING
DECORATIVE STITCHING
EMBROIDERED DECOUPAGE

Refer to pages 21–23 for the *Foundation Piecing* and *Embroidered Decoupage* techniques.

BWD07

### Foundation piecing
Use *Tearaway Magic* printable sheets to print the foundation template for an 8in square **8 Pointed Star** patchwork design from *1,200 Classic Foundations* Perfect Quilt software. Use the photo as a guide to the fabrics used to foundation-piece the square.

### Decorative stitching
Use white thread in the needle and bobbin with *Tearaway Magic* at the back of the stitching and an open-toe foot No 20 to sew a row of decorative stitching around the outside edge of the four dark fabric star points.

Stitch used:

### Embroidered decoupage
Use white thread in the needle and bobbin. Hoop the white nylon organza with *Dissolve Magic* to stitch one **BWD07** lace design.

Center this design in the star and stitch it in place using *Invisa* thread.

Make sure the patchwork block measures $8^1/2$in square. (If yours is smaller or larger than this, you can adjust the width of the black fabric border strips so that when they are joined to the sides of the block, it is a piecing size of $10^1/2$in square.)

From the black fabric, cut two $1^1/2$in x $8^1/2$in strips and then join these to the top and bottom of the patchwork square. Also cut two $1^1/2$in x $10^1/2$in strips and join these to the sides of the block.

Block 8 now measures $10^1/2$in square (piecing size).

BWD08

## TECHNIQUE:
EMBROIDER DIRECTLY ONTO FABRIC USING SELF-ADHESIVE
TEAR-AWAY STABILIZER AND (OPTIONAL) PRINTABLE TEMPLATES

Refer to pages 21–23 for the *Hoop Magic* self-adhesive tear-away stabilizer technique for embroidering directly onto fabric, and (optional) the *Template Magic printable sheets* technique.

### Embroider directly onto fabric using *Hoop Magic* self-adhesive tear-away stabilizer

From the white tone-on-tone fabric, cut an 8$^{1/2}$in x 16$^{1/2}$in fabric strip. Use the fabric-marking pen and ruler to mark vertical and horizontal lines that intersect at the center of the fabric. Use these marked lines with *Hoop Magic* self-adhesive tear-away stabilizer, hooped, to position the fabric over the stabilizer. Center and embroider design **BWD08** vertically on the fabric strip using the photo as a guide to the thread colors used.

### Optional – *Template Magic* printable sheets

If your hoop is not large enough to accommodate design **BWD08**, use the design software to split the design in half lengthwise, so it will fit in your hoop area. Save this new half-design and then send it to the machine. Print this design (twice) on *Template Magic* printable sheets and then use these templates to place the two designs together, centered vertically, on the fabric so that the two designs join and appear as one design. Stitch the two designs.

Make two small bows from the 2yd x $^{1/4}$in red satin ribbon. Once the quilt is completed, these will be attached at each end of the embroidery using a hand-sewing needle and thread.

Block 9 now measures 4$^{1/2}$in x 12$^{1/2}$in (piecing size and maintaining the embroidery centered horizontally in the fabric).

BWD09

## TECHNIQUE:

EMBROIDER DIRECTLY ONTO
FABRIC USING SELF-ADHESIVE
TEAR-AWAY STABILIZER AND
PRINTABLE TEMPLATES

Refer to pages 21–23 for the *Hoop Magic* self-adhesive tear-away stabilizer technique for embroidering directly onto fabric, and the *Template Magic* printable sheets technique.

**Embroider directly onto fabric using *Hoop Magic* self-adhesive tear-away stabilizer and *Template Magic* printable sheets**

From the white tone-on-tone fabric, cut a $12^1/_2$in x $18^1/_2$in fabric strip. Use the fabric-marking pen and ruler to mark vertical and horizontal lines that intersect at the center of the fabric. Use the photo and these marked lines as guides to position the fabric over the hooped *Hoop Magic* self-adhesive tear-away stabilizer. Embroider design **BWD09**, centered vertically, on the fabric strip. Also use the photo as a guide to the thread colors used.

Print design **BWD24** on a *Template Magic* printable sheet. Use the photo as a guide to position this template at the base of the feathered '8' design. Embroider this design as for design **BWD09**.

Block 10 now measures $10^1/_2$in x $16^1/_2$in (piecing size and maintaining the embroidery centered vertically in the fabric).

BWD24

33

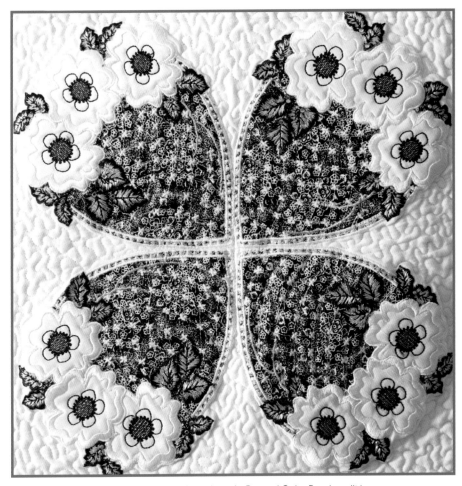

(This block comes from Jenny's *Beyond Color Purple* quilt.)

## TECHNIQUES:

EMBROIDERED DECOUPAGE
EMBROIDER DIRECTLY ONTO
FABRIC USING SELF-ADHESIVE
TEAR-AWAY STABILIZER
(OPTIONAL)

BWD10

Refer to pages 21–23 for the *Embroidered Decoupage* technique, the (optional) *Hoop Magic* self-adhesive tear-away stabilizer technique for embroidering directly onto fabric, and the *Template Magic* printable sheets technique.

From the white tone-on-tone fabric, cut a 14¹/₂in square and then use the fabric-marking pen and quilting ruler to mark vertical, horizontal, and diagonal lines that intersect at the center of the fabric.

### Embroidered decoupage

Use white nylon organza and *Dissolve Magic* to embroider four design **BWD10**, using the photo as a guide to the thread colors used. This design uses the layered embroidered appliqué technique (see Block 6 on page 29 for this technique). For the appliqué use a small black and white patterned fabric for the heart, and plain white fabric for the flowers. (Remember to back the

fabric with *Sheer Magic Plus* to prevent any fraying and puckering of the fabric due to the embroidery.)

Use the photo and marked divide lines as guides to pin and then stitch the four embroidered decoupage designs to the 14¹/₂in square using *Invisa* sheer thread.

### Optional Embroidery

Use the *Template Magic* printable sheets to print four design **BWD10** templates, and then place these centered over the four marked diagonal lines on the 14¹/₂in fabric square, so that the four hearts meet in the center of the fabric. Use the *Hoop Magic* self-adhesive tear-away stabilizer technique along with the templates to embroider the four layered fabric appliqué designs directly onto the fabric.

Block 11 now measures 12¹/₂in square (piecing size and maintaining the embroidery centered in the fabric).

## TECHNIQUE:
### EMBROIDER DIRECTLY ONTO FABRIC USING SELF-ADHESIVE TEAR-AWAY STABILIZER

Refer to pages 21–23 for the *Hoop Magic* self-adhesive tear-away stabilizer technique for embroidering directly onto fabric.

Embroider directly onto fabric using *Hoop Magic* self-adhesive tear-away stabilizer.

From the white tone-on-tone fabric, cut an 8$\frac{1}{2}$in x 16$\frac{1}{2}$in fabric strip and then use the fabric-marking pen and quilting ruler to mark vertical and horizontal lines that intersect at the center of the strip.

Embroider design **BWD11** centered vertically on the fabric strip. Use the *Hoop Magic* self-adhesive tear-away stabilizer in the hoop and the marked lines to position the fabric over the stabilizer in the hoop, and then embroider the design using black thread.

Cut the block to 4in x 12$\frac{1}{2}$in, keeping the embroidery centered.

From the black fabric, cut a 1in x 12$\frac{1}{2}$in strip and then join this to the top of the 4in x 12$\frac{1}{2}$in embroidered strip.

Block 12 now measures 4$\frac{1}{2}$in x 12$\frac{1}{2}$in (piecing size and maintaining the embroidery centered horizontally in the fabric).

**This block completes the second block row (Blocks 6 to 12).**

You are now halfway through the blocks for the *Black & White Dreams* quilt.

BWD11

## TECHNIQUE:
EMBROIDER DIRECTLY ONTO FABRIC USING
SELF-ADHESIVE TEAR-AWAY STABILIZER

Refer to pages 21–23 for the *Hoop Magic* self-adhesive tear-away stabilizer technique for embroidering directly onto fabric.

### Embroider directly onto fabric using *Hoop Magic* self-adhesive tear-away stabilizer

From the white tone-on-tone fabric, cut an $8^1/2$in x $14^1/2$in strip and then use the fabric-marking pen and quilting ruler to mark vertical and horizontal lines that intersect at the center of the fabric. Use these lines and *Hoop Magic* self-adhesive tear-away stabilizer, hooped, to position the fabric vertically in the hoop to embroider design **BWD12**. Use the photo as a guide to thread colors used.

Block 13 now measures $6^1/2$in x $12^1/2$in (horizontal piecing size and maintaining the embroidery centered horizontally in the fabric).

BWD12

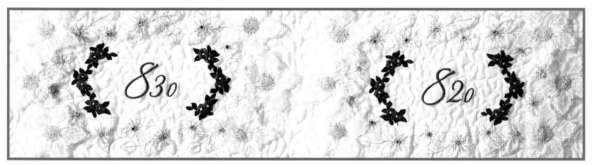

## TECHNIQUES:
EMBROIDER DIRECTLY ONTO
FABRIC USING SELF-ADHESIVE
TEAR-AWAY STABILIZER
THREE-DIMENSIONAL
EMBROIDERED DECOUPAGE

Refer to pages 21–23 for the *Hoop Magic* self-adhesive tear-away stabilizer technique for embroidering directly onto the fabric, and the *Three-dimensional embroidered decoupage* technique.

### Embroider directly onto fabric using *Hoop Magic* self-adhesive tear-away stabilizer

From the white tone-on-tone fabric, cut an 8½in x 24½in strip and then use the fabric-marking pen and quilting ruler to mark vertical and horizontal lines that intersect at the center of the fabric. On the 24½in horizontal line, measure out 5½in on each side of the center and mark it. Use the points to mark vertical lines that pass through these marks and intersect the horizontal line. Label these intersections A and B. These intersecting lines are used as positional lines to embroider designs **BWD13** and **BWD14**.

Use intersection A, the marked lines and the *Hoop Magic* self-adhesive tear-away stabilizer, hooped, to position the fabric vertically in the hoop to embroider design **BWD13**. Use the photo as a guide to the thread colors used. Repeat for intersection B to embroider design **BWD14**.

Use the heating tool to secure a clear heat-activated crystal in the center of each flower in both designs.

### Three-dimensional embroidered decoupage

Use white nylon organza and *Dissolve Magic* to embroider 12 **BWD31** designs. (You may choose to use your software to combine these in one hoop area and then color-sort the combination design, save it, and send it to the machine.) Use white thread in the needle and bobbin for the flower outlines and silver for the centers.

Use the photo as a guide to position and pin three of these flowers on each horizontal side of designs **BWD13** and **BWD14**. Use *Invisa* thread to freehand-stitch around the centers only of the flowers to attach them to the block.

Block 14 now measures 6½in x 22½in (horizontal piecing size and maintaining the embroidery centered horizontally in the fabric).

BWD13

BWD14

BWD31

## CHECKERBOARD NO 2

### TECHNIQUES:

FOUNDATION PIECING
DECORATIVE STITCHING
EMBROIDERED DECOUPAGE

Refer to pages 21–23 for the *Foundation Piecing* and *Embroidered Decoupage* techniques.

BWD15

### Foundation piecing

Use *Tearaway Magic* printable sheets to print the foundation template for a 9in square **Checkerboard No 2** patchwork design from *Easy Strip Piecing* Perfect Quilt software. Use the photo as a guide to the fabrics used to foundation-piece the square.

### Decorative stitching

Use white thread in the needle and bobbin with *Tearaway Magic* at the back of the stitching and an open-toe foot No 20 to sew two intersecting diagonal rows of decorative stitching that extend from corner to corner of the block.

Stitch used:

Also sew two lines of triple-stitch (using black thread) that are parallel to and on both sides of the decorative stitch. The triple-stitch rows are sewn in the seamlines of the patchwork, using the photo as a guide, to form a center square on point.

### Embroidered decoupage

Use white nylon organza, *Dissolve Magic* and white thread to embroider lace design **BWD15**. Pin and then stitch this design to the center of the block using *Invisa* sheer thread, stitching around the outside edge of the design.

From the black fabric, cut two 1in x 9½in strips and join these to the top and bottom of the **Checkerboard No 2** block. Also cut two 1in x 10½in strips and join these to the sides of the block.

Block 15 now measures 10½in square (piecing size).

## TECHNIQUES:
EMBROIDER DIRECTLY ONTO
FABRIC USING SELF-ADHESIVE
TEAR-AWAY STABILIZER AND
PRINTABLE TEMPLATES
THREE-DIMENSIONAL
EMBROIDERED DECOUPAGE

Refer to pages 21–23 for the *Hoop Magic* self-adhesive tear-away stabilizer technique for embroidering directly onto the fabric, and the *Three-dimensional embroidered decoupage* technique.

From the white tone-on-tone fabric, cut a 12$^1$/$_2$in square and then use the fabric-marking pen and quilting ruler to mark a centered 10$^1$/$_2$in square. Also mark diagonal lines that intersect at the center of the fabric.

### Embroider directly onto fabric using *Hoop Magic* self-adhesive tear-away stabilizer and *Template Magic* printable sheets
Use a *Tearaway Magic* printable sheet to print a template for design **BWD16**. Place this template centered diagonally in the bottom left corner of the fabric so that the long side of the feathered

triangle is aligned with and parallel to the opposite marked diagonal line. The right-angle sides of the design should sit within and be parallel to the two sides of the marked 10$^1$/$_2$in square.

Use the design template, black thread, and *Hoop Magic* self-adhesive tear-away stabilizer, hooped, to position the fabric diagonally on the hoop and embroider design **BWD16**.

### Three-dimensional embroidered decoupage
Use black nylon organza, *Dissolve Magic*, and black thread to embroider the flower and leaves section of design **BWD17**. Use white nylon organza for the single flower part of the design, with white thread for the flower petals and silver for the center.

Use the photo as a guide to position and then pin the black organza flower and leaves. Next, use *Invisa* thread to freehand-stitch along the stems, leaf veins and around the center of the flower only. Layer the white organza flower over the black one so that the petals are offset, and stitch it around the center only to attach it to the black flower. Use the heating tool to set clear heat-activated crystals in the center of the flower.

Cut the block to 10$^1$/$_2$in square. From the black fabric, cut a 2$^1$/$_2$in x 10$^1$/$_2$in strip and then join this to the right side of the block.

Block 16 now measures 10$^1$/$_2$in x 12$^1$/$_2$in (piecing size).

BWD16

BWD17

BWD18

BWD22

## TECHNIQUES:
### DECORATIVE STITCHING
### EMBROIDERED DECOUPAGE
### THREE-DIMENSIONAL
### EMBROIDERED DECOUPAGE

Refer to pages 21–23 for the *Embroidered Decoupage* and *Three-dimensional embroidered decoupage* techniques.

From the white tone-on-tone fabric, cut a 12¹/₂in square and then use the fabric-marking pen and quilting ruler to mark vertical and horizontal lines that intersect at the center of the fabric. Use a compass to also mark a circle with a 4in radius in the center of the fabric. Mark a 1in vertical/horizontal grid inside the marked circle using the marked divide lines as starting points.

### Decorative stitching
Use black thread in the needle and bobbin with *Tearaway Magic* at the back of the stitching and an open-toe foot No 20 to sew over the grid lines, stopping and starting at the marked circle.

Use a triple-stitch for the vertical lines and a decorative stitch for the horizontal lines.

Also sew around the circle using a decorative stitch.

### Embroidered decoupage
Use white nylon organza and *Dissolve Magic* to embroider combination design **BWD18** using the photo as a guide to thread colors used. Also use the photo as a guide to arrange a mirrored rose spray and leaves on left-to-right diagonally opposite sides of the decorative stitched circle. Use *Invisa* thread to stitch around the outside edge of the sprays and leaves to attach them to the block.

### Three-dimensional
*embroidered decoupage*
Use white nylon organza and *Dissolve Magic* to embroider combination design **BWD22** using white thread in the needle and bobbin for the leaf circle and flower petals and silver thread for the center of the freestanding flower.

Center the leaf circle in the decorative stitched circle. Pin it and then attach it to the fabric around the leaf outline only. Layer the flower over the center of the leaf garland and attach it around the center of the flower only.

Apply clear heat-activated crystals to the flower center using a heating tool.

Block 17 is now cut to measure a piecing size of 10¹/₂in square (maintaining the embroidery centered diagonally in the fabric).

## TECHNIQUES:

EMBROIDER DIRECTLY ONTO
FABRIC USING SELF-ADHESIVE
TEAR-AWAY STABILIZER AND
PRINTABLE TEMPLATES
APPLIQUE

Refer to pages 21–23 for the technique to embroider directly onto fabric using *Hoop Magic* self-adhesive tear-away stabilizer and *Template Magic* printable sheets.

## BLOCK 18

Embroider directly onto fabric using *Hoop Magic* self-adhesive tear-away stabilizer and *Template Magic* printable sheets.

From the white tone-on-tone fabric, cut a $10^1/2$in x $16^1/2$in fabric strip. Use the fabric-marking pen and quilting ruler to mark vertical and horizontal lines that intersect at the center of the fabric.

### Appliqué

Use a hot steam iron to press an 8in x 11in piece of gray and silver fabric to a matching sized piece of *Web Magic*

BWD19

41

Place on fold

*Magic* pressure-sensitive double-sided fusible web, wrong side of fabric to fusible side of web. Iron from both the fabric side and the protective backing side of the web.

Use the tracing paper and lead pencil to trace around the heart pattern on this page and then use the paper scissors to cut it out. Lay the heart pattern over the fabric backed with the web and then trace around the outside and the inside scallops of the heart and cut it out. Remove the backing paper from the web and center the heart appliqué in the block. As the web is pressure-sensitive it will stay in place on the fabric without being pinned. (It can also be replaced as many times as needed for accurate placement.) Use a hot steam iron to press the appliqué heart to the fabric block.

Use black thread in the needle, an open-toe foot No 20, and a narrow pin-

stitch to sew around both the outside and inside scalloped edge of the heart.

**NOTE: The center of the heart will be quilted with a $1/2$in diagonal grid when the quilt is pieced and quilted, and clear heat-activated crystals will be applied to every grid intersection using a heating tool.**

### Embroider appliqué directly onto fabric using *Hoop Magic* self-adhesive tear-away stabilizer and *Template Magic* printable sheets.

Use *Tearaway Magic* printable sheets to print a template for design **BWD19** and **BWD19** (mirrored horizontally). Use the photo as a guide to place a template on each side of the heart. Use the design template and *Hoop Magic* self-adhesive tear-away stabilizer, hooped, to position the fabric on the hoop to embroider design **BWD19** on the right side of the appliqué heart, with black fabric for the appliqué insert and using

the photo as a guide to thread colors used. Repeat for the mirrored template on the left side of the heart using a small black and white patterned fabric for the appliqué insert.

Cut the embroidered appliqué block to $8^1/2$in x 14in (maintaining the embroidery centered vertically in the fabric). Cut a 1in x $8^1/2$in strip of block fabric and then stitch this to the bottom of the block.

Block 18 now measures $8^1/2$in x $14^1/2$in (piecing size).

### BLOCK NO 19

From a favorite white background fabric with an interesting black print (for example, one with butterflies on it), cut an $8^1/2$in x $4^1/2$in strip.

Block 19 now measures $8^1/2$in x $4^1/2$in (piecing size).

**This block completes the third block row (Blocks 13 to 19).**

You are now three-quarters of the way through the blocks.

## DUTCHMAN'S PUZZLE

### TECHNIQUES:
FOUNDATION PIECING
DECORATIVE STITCHING
EMBROIDERED DECOUPAGE

Refer to pages 21–23 for the *Foundation Piecing* and *Embroidered Decoupage* techniques.

### Foundation piecing
Use *Tearaway Magic* printable sheets to print the foundation template for a 12in square **Dutchman's Puzzle** patchwork design from *1,200 Classic Foundations Perfect Quilt* software. Use the photo as a guide to the fabrics used to foundation-piece the square.

### Decorative stitching
Use black thread to stitch on white background fabric and white thread to stitch on black background fabric (matching needle and bobbin thread) with *Tearaway Magic* at the back of the stitching and an open-toe foot No 20 to sew a decorative stitch over the seamline on the right-angle points of the eight triangles.

Stitch used:

### Embroidered decoupage
Use white nylon organza and *Dissolve Magic* to embroider four lace designs **BWD20** using white thread in the needle and bobbin. Pin and then stitch these four designs centered between the four black triangles so that the designs point to and meet in the center of the block. Use *Invisa* sheer thread, stitching around the outside edge of each design.

Block 20 now measures $12^{1}/_{2}$in square (piecing size).

BWD20

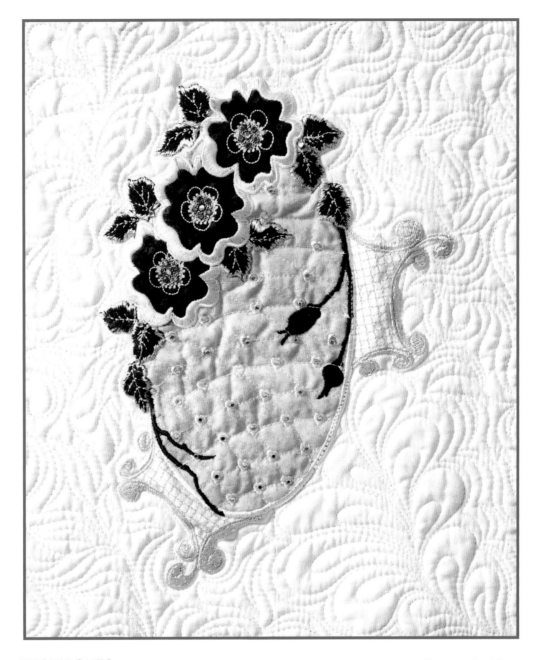

## TECHNIQUES:
EMBROIDER DIRECTLY ONTO
FABRIC USING SELF-ADHESIVE
TEAR-AWAY STABILIZER AND
EMBROIDERED APPLIQUE

BWD21

Refer to pages 21–23 for the technique to embroider directly onto fabric using *Hoop Magic* self-adhesive tear-away stabilizer and *Template Magic* printable sheets.

### Embroidered appliqué directly onto fabric using *Hoop Magic* self-adhesive tear-away stabilizer

From the white tone-on-tone fabric, cut a 14¹/2in x 16¹/2in fabric strip. Use the fabric-marking pen and quilting ruler to mark vertical and horizontal lines that intersect at the center of the fabric.

Vertically center the fabric over *Hoop Magic* self-adhesive tear-away stabilizer hooped, to embroider design **BWD21**, vertically centered on the fabric.

Use the gray and silver fabric backed with *Sheer Magic Plus* for the oval appliqué fabric insert, and black fabric for the flower appliqué fabric insert (referring to Block 6 on page 29). Embroider design **BWD21** centered in the fabric, using the photo as a guide to the thread colors used.

Block 21 now measures 10¹/2in x 12¹/2in (piecing size and maintaining the embroidery centered vertically in the fabric).

## TECHNIQUES:
EMBROIDER DIRECTLY ONTO
FABRIC USING SELF-ADHESIVE
TEAR-AWAY STABILIZER AND
(OPTIONAL) PRINTABLE
TEMPLATES

Refer to pages 21–23 for the *Hoop Magic* self-adhesive tear-away stabilizer technique for embroidering directly onto fabric, and (optional) the *Template Magic* printable sheets technique.

### Embroider directly onto fabric using *Hoop Magic* self-adhesive tear-away stabilizer

From the white tone-on-tone fabric, cut an 8$\frac{1}{2}$in x 14$\frac{1}{2}$in fabric strip. Use the fabric-marking pen and ruler to mark vertical and horizontal lines that intersect at the center of the fabric. Use these marked lines with *Hoop Magic* self-adhesive tear-away stabilizer, hooped, to position the fabric over the

BWD23

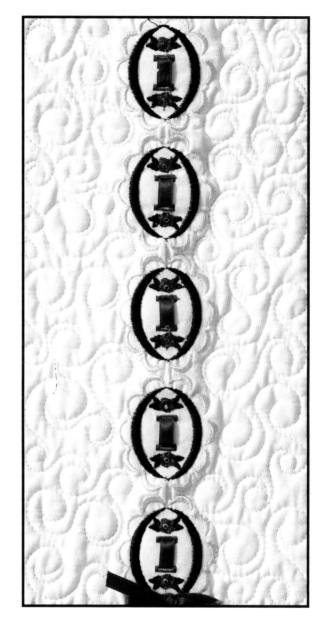

stabilizer to embroider design **BWD23** centered vertically on the fabric strip, and use the photo as a guide to the thread colors used.

### Optional – *Template Magic* printable sheets

If your hoop is not large enough to accommodate design **BWD23**, use the design software to split the design into two sections (one has three scallops and the other has two), so it will fit in your hoop area. Save these two new designs and then send them to the machine. Print the two new designs on *Template Magic* printable sheets and then use these templates to place the two designs together, vertically centered on the fabric,

so that the two designs join and appear as one design. Stitch the two designs.

Use small sharp scissors to carefully cut the 10 buttonholes in the center of the scallops and then use a bodkin to thread the $\frac{1}{4}$in red satin ribbon through the buttonholes, leaving a tail at the beginning and at the end to be caught in the seam. A small bow is attached at the bottom end of the ribbon after the block is pieced and quilted. Clear heat-activated crystals are also applied to the center of the little flowers using a heating tool.

Block 22 now measures 6$\frac{1}{2}$in x 12$\frac{1}{2}$in (piecing size and maintaining the embroidery centered vertically in the fabric).

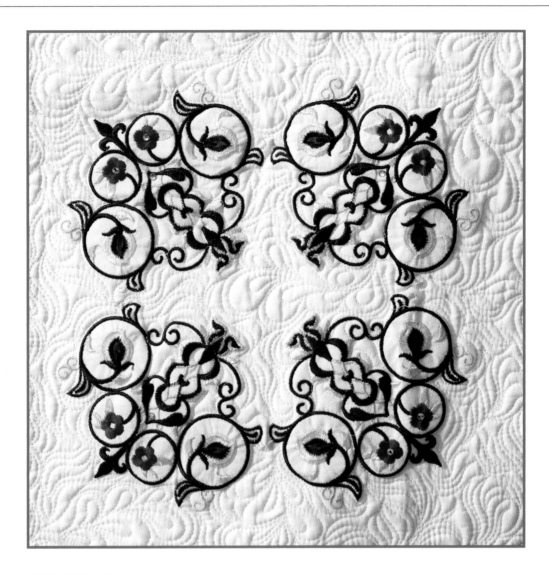

## TECHNIQUES:
EMBROIDER DIRECTLY ONTO
FABRIC USING SELF-ADHESIVE
TEAR-AWAY STABILIZER AND
PRINTABLE TEMPLATES

BWD25

Refer to pages 21–23 for the *Hoop Magic* self-adhesive tear-away stabilizer technique for embroidering directly onto fabric, and the *Template Magic* printable sheets technique.

### Embroider directly onto fabric using *Hoop Magic* self-adhesive tear-away stabilizer and *Template Magic* printable sheets

From the white tone-on-tone fabric, cut a 14¹/₂in square. Use the fabric-marking pen and ruler to mark vertical, horizontal, and diagonal lines that intersect at the center of the fabric.

Use two sheets of *Template Magic* to print designs **BWD25** and **BWD25** (mirrored horizontally). Use the photo as a guide to place a printed template, centered vertically, on the left and right side of the fabric so that the designs

point to the center and just touch at the marked divide lines. Each design should then also be centered over the marked diagonal lines.

Use the marked lines, the printed templates and *Hoop Magic* self-adhesive tear-away stabilizer, hooped, to position the fabric vertically over the stabilizer to embroider design **BWD25** (left side of the design). Use the photo as a guide to the thread colors used. Repeat for design **BWD25** (mirrored horizontally) for the right side of the fabric.

Block 23 now measures 12¹/₂in square (piecing size and maintaining the embroidery centered in the fabric).

**This block completes the fourth and final block row (Blocks 20 to 23).**

**Congratulations! You have completed all the quilt blocks for *Black & White Dreams*!**

## PUTTING THE QUILT TOGETHER

NOTE: Remember that this is a 'scrappy' quilt, so if any of your measurements differ from the ones given, just add fabric to or remove it from the blocks, to match the measurements provided.

### Strip-piecing

**1** All construction uses construction thread in the needle and bobbin and a $1/4$in patchwork foot.

**2** When you are cutting the fabrics for strip-piecing, and then cross-cutting the strip-pieced fabric for the sashing strips, you need to be very accurate as small variances will alter the width and length of these squares and units.

**3** Use the rotary cutter, self-healing cutting mat, and quilting ruler to cut $2^{1}/_{2}$in strips across the width of the fabric of the 18 fat quarters of black and white patterned fabric for the sashing strips.

**4** Lay these $2^{1}/_{2}$in fabric strips out in an 18-fabric sequence, making sure you alternate light and dark fabrics, and then strip-piece these fabric strips together, repeating the 18-fabric sequence until all the lengths have been pieced.

**5** Press all the seams flat.

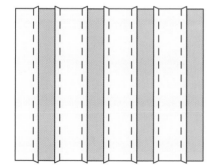

TIP: Run the point of the iron up every second fabric strip from the back of the fabric. This flattens the seams to each side of the strip, as shown in the diagram above.

**6** Cross-cut the striped pieced fabric into $2^{1}/_{2}$in strips. You will need a total of at least 285, $2^{1}/_{2}$in squares. These strips can now be joined (or unpicked) into piecing units of a specified number of $2^{1}/_{2}$in squares.

### Joining the blocks into rows

NOTE: Refer to the quilt layout diagram on page 49 and the photo on page 19 at all times as you piece the blocks and then join them into rows.

**7 Block row No 1**
– Join Block 2 vertically to the right side of Block 1
– Join Block 4 horizontally to the top of Block 5
– Make four units of five $2^{1}/_{2}$in squares for sashing strips.
Join the three pieced blocks into a row:
– Starting and finishing the block row with a five-square sashing unit, join the first block (pieced Blocks 1 and 2) with a sashing unit to Block 3, and then with a sashing unit to the third block (pieced Blocks 4 and 5).

**8 Block row No 2**
– Join a unit of four $2^{1}/_{2}$in squares to the bottom of Block 6
– Join a unit of three $2^{1}/_{2}$in squares to the right side of Block 7
– Join a unit of five $2^{1}/_{2}$in squares to the left side of Block 8
– Join a unit of six $2^{1}/_{2}$in squares to the top of horizontal Block 9
– Join Block 7 to the bottom of Block 6, and Block 9 to the bottom of Block 8
– Join pieced Blocks 6 and 7 vertically to pieced Blocks 8 and 9
– Join Block 12 horizontally to Block 11
– Make four units of eight $2^{1}/_{2}$in squares for sashing strips.
Join the three pieced blocks into a row:
– Starting and finishing the block row with an eight-square sashing unit, join the first block (pieced Blocks 6 to 9) vertically with a sashing unit to Block 10, and then with a sashing unit to the third block (pieced Blocks 11 and 12).

**9 Block row No 3**
– Join a unit of three $2^{1}/_{2}$in squares to the right side of Block 13
– Join a unit of five $2^{1}/_{2}$in squares to the right of Block 15
– Join a unit of five $2^{1}/_{2}$in squares to the left side of Block 17
– Join pieced Block 13 vertically to Block 14
– Join Blocks 15 to 17 vertically together
– Join a piecing unit of 18, $2^{1}/_{2}$in squares to the bottom of pieced Blocks 13 and 14, and then join pieced Blocks 15 to 17 to the bottom of the 18-square piecing unit
– Join Block 19 horizontally to the bottom of Block 18
– Make three units of nine $2^{1}/_{2}$in squares for sashing strips.
Join the two pieced blocks into a row:
– Starting and finishing the block row with a nine-square sashing unit, join the first block (pieced Blocks 13 to 17) vertically with a sashing unit to the second block (pieced Blocks 18 and 19).

**10 Block row No 4**
– Make five units of six $2^{1}/_{2}$in squares for sashing strips.
Join the four blocks into a row:
– Starting and finishing with (and with each one separated by) a six-square sashing unit, join Blocks 20 to 23 together.

### Joining the block rows together

**11** Make five units of 25, $2^{1}/_{2}$in squares to join the block rows together.

**12** Join block rows No 1 to No 4 together with the five 25-square units, starting and finishing with a 25-square unit.

## MITERED BORDERS
### Cutting

1 From the white tone-on-tone fabric (backed with *Sheer Magic Plus*), cut:
– two 10in x 94in strips for the top and bottom borders
– two 10in x 94in strips for the sides.

2 Use the fabric-marking pen and quilting ruler to mark the borders with vertical and horizontal lines that intersect at the center of each border strip.

3 Use the layout diagram on page 49, referring in particular to the red embroidery positional crosses marked on the borders. Use the fabric-marking pen and ruler to mark these positions (using the measurements marked on the layout diagram) with vertical lines that intersect at the long horizontal lines on each of the border strips.

### Embroidery
#### Quilted feather design
Embroider directly onto the fabric using *Hoop Magic* self-adhesive tear-away stabilizer and *Template Magic* printable sheets

4 Use the design software to print placement templates on the *Template Magic* printable sheets for the following embroidered quilting designs from the *Galleria* CD:

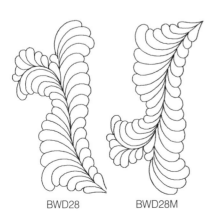

BWD28       BWD28M

BWD30       BWD30M

BWD29

5 Use the paper scissors to roughly cut out each template, and then use the photo as a guide to combine the five templates, on the border fabric strip, into one feather design that is centered over one of the positioning crosses marked on a border fabric strip.

6 The center feather quilting embroidery should be stitched first on the side border strips, and then the ones on either side of the center.

7 Refer to pages 21–23 for more detailed directions on how to use the printed templates and *Hoop Magic* self-adhesive tear-away stabilizer for easy and accurate placement of embroidery designs.

8 The border fabric strips are placed vertically over the stabilizer in the hoop, with the designs embroidered vertically.

9 Use black thread to embroider the five combination feather designs in the following sequence: **BWD29**, **BWD28**, **BWD30**, and then repeat for the other side of the design using **BWD28M**, and **BWD30M**.

10 Embroider two feather designs (on each side of the center for the top and bottom borders, and three evenly spaced feather designs on the side borders).

11 Embroider **B E R N I N A** in black thread and with a font of your choice, using a printed placement template to center the embroidery in the bottom border fabric strip.

### Three-dimensional *embroidered decoupage*
Refer to pages 21–23 for more detailed directions on this technique.

12 Use red and black nylon organza matching needle and bobbin thread, *Dissolve Magic*, and red, black, and silver metallic thread for the three-dimensional *embroidered decoupage* flowers and leaves for the border strips. These can be embroidered now but will not be stitched to the borders until after the quilting is complete.

13 Embroider 30 flowers without centers, **BWD27**, using black thread and nylon organza, and 30 flowers with centers, **BWD26**, using red thread and nylon organza, and silver metallic thread for the centers.

14 Embroider 20 (five sets of four) leaves, **BWD32**, using black thread and nylon organza.

15 The 60 flowers are layered as in Block 1 (see page 24), with red flower sitting over black flower, petals offset and held together around the center using *Invisa* thread, and a freehand straight stitch. Now put the flowers and leaves to one side.

### FINISHING IT OFF
16 Attach the borders to the quilt, mitering (using your preferred method) the corners as you go. Press the quilt top.

17 Either use a hot steam iron to fuse the *Quilt Magic* lightweight fusible batting to the back of your quilt (you may even use two layers if you want more loft to your quilting) or use *Matilda's Own* cotton batting. Have your quilt quilted as you wish using the 81in x 97in backing fabric.

**18** Cut your quilt to a finished size of 69in x 85in. From the black fabric, cut 2¹/₂in strips across the width of the fabric to join on the bias for a total length of 320in. Bind, sign, and then date your quilt.

**19** Use the quilt photo on page 19 as a guide. Position, pin, and then stitch the flowers and leaves to the quilt borders using *Invisa* thread. Attach the leaves by stitching down the leaf veins and stems only, and the flowers around the centers only.

**20** Congratulations! Don't you feel proud that you have now completed your *Black & White Dreams* quilt. What an awesome way to celebrate the launch of the Bernina *8-series* machines – surely this is what dreams are made of.

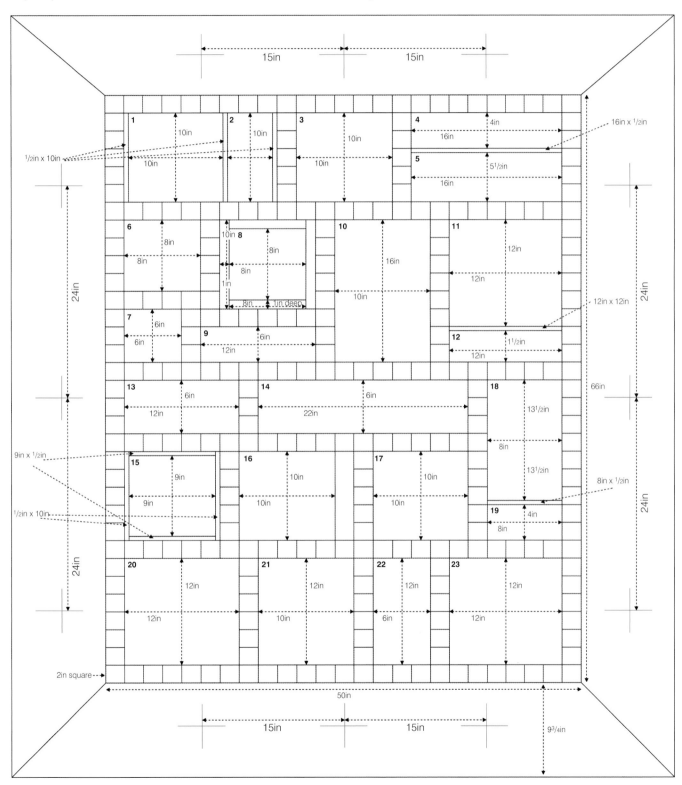

FINISHED SIZE OF QUILT – 69in x 85in (175cm x 216cm)

TRUDY BILLINGSLEY
SYDNEY, NSW, AUSTRALIA

trudy billingsley

Trudy loves the brilliant colors of the Australian landscape and the character of its people, both of which have a strong influence on her working artistic style.

Memories and sketches from numerous journeys and family vacations have served as an endless source of design ideas for Trudy's creative wearable art, wall quilts, and fashion accessories.

THE VERY DIVERSE AUSTRALIAN ENVIRONMENT and its people form an important part of Trudy's artistic impressions of the magnificent Australian terrain. Trudy enjoys using objects she has either found or collected, such as memorabilia, documents, stamps, buttons, beads, uniforms, and sketches, which she uses as overlay and cutback work to embellish and texture the surface of her work.

Trudy's techniques have been self-developed and simplified so as to incorporate both large and small objects in her works of art. By using a wide variety of collectable fabric fragments such as silks, cottons, chintz, wools, and threads, Trudy then manipulates and molds these materials to create her uniquely textured signature designs. These molded materials are then used to enhance and embellish Trudy's garments, accessories, and fiber art works.

As well as Trudy's innovative garments, she also designs and personally crafts one-of-a-kind fashion accessories such as designer scarves, shawls, and glorious evening bags. These are highly sought after and carried in exclusive boutiques and designer stores, feeding Trudy's creativity and keeping her sewing machine busy.

Trudy is a well-known and respected international tutor, having conducted numerous workshops for corporate organizations as well as private student groups. She has traveled all over Australia, Japan, Germany, and New Zealand, and delights her eager students with her vast knowledge on how to use a sewing machine to design from nature and incorporate it into both wearable art and surface collages.

**You can contact Trudy via email (geoff@billingsley.com.au) for more information on her classes and fiber art works.**

# SEE ME SWING
*Trudy Billingsley*

The inspiration for this piece came from Trudy's love of free-flowing asymmetrical designs. Having to abandon her preferred color palette of earthy tones, it was a true challenge for Trudy to be asked to use an unfamiliar red, black, white, and silver color scheme. Trudy chose machine tucks and folds, edged with silver braid and corded with white ribbon, to create the fabric for her wrap. She then designed machine embroidered figure 8s which she applied to the panels on the wrap with buttons to create the perception of floridity and movement.

JENNY BOWKER
CANBERRA, ACT, AUSTRALIA

# jenny bowker

Jenny (who has a background in science) is an internationally acclaimed quilt artist, tutor, and exhibition judge who has been involved in textiles since 1997 when she graduated from university with a Bachelor of Arts Degree (Visual). It was at this time that Jenny decided to make just one quilt!

Her contemporary work is usually based on science or women's issues, however Jenny is moving toward melding her fine art with textiles. Loving the way patterns come into so many parts of our lives, Jenny often includes geometrical piecing in her work as it keeps her technically on her toes and provides a key for traditional quilters to link with her work.

JENNY WANTED TO MAKE something special for Bernina as she feels enormous gratitude for the assistance and support given to her by them over the years. The good people at Bernina have lent Jenny machines in locations all over the world and flown her to classes all over the world. They even had a machine delivered to a hospital hostel for Jenny when her daughter was badly burned and Jenny had a quilting deadline to meet.

Wanting something in her style, as requested by Bernina, Jenny found it hard to meet the red, black, white, and silver color challenge, as her artistic style is pictorial and representational. She wanted to create something that would fascinate and hold a person's gaze, to pull them in for a closer look. Jenny also wanted something that incorporated an innovative skill – the sort of technique that might make people wonder how it was achieved.

Having lived for eleven years in Arabic and Islamic countries (as she joined her husband in his diplomatic work for the Australian Department of Foreign Affairs and Trade), Jenny developed a love of the Middle East, and so much of the subject matter in her quilts reflects this fascination.

The '8' as a theme was a problem, however, and Jenny is aware that she did not adopt this theme in the way that perhaps the others did – but the stone walls of the buildings in Cairo have red numbers on them now, even the actual mosque which did not have one before!

*You Can Make Anything with a Bernina – Anywhere or Anyone* is made with cotton fabrics, some commercial and a few hand-dyed, and the batting is *Matilda's Own* wool-mix. Jenny used *Mettler* and *Signature* threads along with silver foiled jersey, which is usually used for dance costumes. This type of fabric will ladder if it is cut, so Jenny heat-cut the intricate mosque door design (using a soldering iron with a fine tip) after she had stitched it.

As a tutor, Jenny knows of no greater delight than to offer the tools to a quilting artist to access their ideas to create original art and then to see these dreams become reality.

**You can contact Jenny for information on her blog (http://jennybowker.blogspot.com), her website (http://www.jennybowker.com/), or flickr (http://www.flickr.com/photos/jennybowker/).**

# YOU CAN MAKE ANYTHING WITH A BERNINA – ANYWHERE OR ANYONE
## *Jenny Bowker*

Mohamed Sa'ad stands in front of the beautiful old door of the mosque in Cairo, Egypt, where for many years he sang the call to prayer as a muezzin. His voice is now gone and the mosque is under repair, but he still remains as the caretaker, living there with his wife and daughter. The address is 8 Sharia Khayamiya (the Tentmakers Street).

EDITOR'S NOTE:

Jenny's quilt was personally purchased by Claude Dreyer of Bernina Switzerland (see photo on opposite page) to hang in his office at Bernina headquarters. For four years Jenny lived in Cairo as the wife of the Australian Ambassador to Egypt and this is where she met Mohamed, who became a good friend. Jenny returned there recently to seek out her friend in order to give him a monetary gift, which she felt was owed to him, as it was his image used on the quilt. This gift allowed Mohamed to acquire a small flat for him and his family in which to live (rather than at the mosque).

Jenny, your quilt is amazing and your story even more beautiful. Thank you for sharing it with me.

CHERYL BRIDGART
ADELAIDE, SA, AUSTRALIA

CHERYL LIVES IN THE CBD OF ADELAIDE, in a 150-year-old historic building that was a horse stable, built by Osmond Gilles (who introduced merino sheep into SA) in 1850. For those intrigued with Australian history, Osmond arrived in Australia on the ship *Buffalo* with Governor Hindmarsh. In its past life this building has served as stables for horses of Pikes Brewery, the 'Police Greys' (horses) and an art gallery and offices for one of South Australia's largest cattle stations, Beltana. Now known as Beltana House, these stables serve as Cheryl's home, gallery, and studio, and still retain its original architecture. In keeping with a stable, it also allows vehicles to drive (as opposed to riding a horse) into the open stable area.

Cheryl has a Bachelor of Education and an Advanced Diploma of Fine Art, both of which stemmed from her earliest childhood love of drawing, painting, and sewing.

The irresistible passion of both art and sewing quickly merged and soon Cheryl began 'drawing' animals and faces with her sewing machine. Creating artworks on fabric has become a lifelong passion and has enabled Cheryl to turn her obsession with textile art into a full-time career.

As a textile artist, Cheryl aims to create a new art form of freestyle vivid needle-painting to visually express her passion for machine embroidery, dreams, and life. Although she has a fine art training, she is a self-taught machine embroiderer (something she is passionate about), and enjoys developing her own personal style and techniques.

Machine embroidery has become an extension of Cheryl's love and talent for sketching, produced pictures, and wearable art, which become richer and more tactile with stitching. Her skill with a sewing machine using the needle as a paintbrush and thread as her palette allows Cheryl to create very detailed images on blank canvas (no under-drawing, paint, dye, or computers are used) using stitching only.

Over the years Cheryl discovered that a limited thread palette gave greater scope and dimension to her thread paintings. Drawing on the color theories used by the Impressionists (in particular Claude Monet), the juxtaposition of color (placing one over the top of another) can change its appearance, resulting in the creation of a wider optical color range. So now, by using fewer colors and combining them with stitching and crosshatching, Cheryl finds she can create a richer surface to her textile art pieces. Cheryl finds it exciting as she continues experimenting with new innovations and techniques that constantly enhance her wall works and wearable art.

Cheryl's creative textile art pieces have been widely published and exhibited throughout Australia and internationally, including in America, the UK, Japan, and New Zealand, resulting in lecture and workshop tours. Her work has been published in such prestigious magazines and books as *Masters of Their Craft, Tradition and Innovation in Contemporary Decorative Arts* by Norris Ioannou, and *Machine Embroidery Inspirations from Australian Artists* by Kristen Dibbs. As well as all this, Cheryl has been a guest on such popular TV programs as *Postcards* and *Better Homes and Gardens*. Cheryl's recognition in the art world extends to having her textile art included in exhibitions at The Powerhouse Museum in Sydney, Plescher/Palmer in the USA, the Madeira International Art Collection in the UK, Hemeji in Japan, and Australia's Victorian State Opera.

As the winner of The Australian Tourism Commission/Qantas/Australian Arts Council's 'Dreamtime *96 National Billy Can Art Award*', Cheryl was honored that her art was used to promote Australian tourism worldwide.

Cheryl loves to paint and is a prolific drawer, but she finds nothing can display the fine qualities, nuances, and feelings she wants to engender more than the stitch. Machine embroidery allows Cheryl to turn her dreams and feelings into contemporary, tactile diaries that reflect her passion for life and color.

If you are down that way, Cheryl would welcome you to her gallery at 364 Carrington Street, Adelaide in South Australia. It is well worth the visit.

**You can contact Cheryl via email (cheryl@bridgart.com.au) or visit her website (www.bridgart.com.au) for information on her upcoming exhibitions and lecture tours.**

cheryl bridgart

# AUSTRALIA – 8 AUSSIE ICONS
## *Cheryl Bridgart*

The blue map of Australia reminds Australians that we are on an island, encircled by sea. The face represents the people; the Opera House, Australia's architectural marvel, represents our creativity; and the red '8' encircles man and our creative world, which is surrounded by the unique natural beauty of Australia's flora and fauna.

Cheryl used freehand thread painting (with no assistance or any guidelines) for the face, which is rendered with thread only, backed with batting and then stitched to the base canvas to add a relief to the surface. Tiny pieces of red silk are stitched into the number '8' and on the birds' feathers to create texture. Touches of blue brocade are collaged at the base while the rest of the work has been drawn purely with needle and thread.

EILEEN CAMPBELL
KEW, VIC., AUSTRALIA

eileen campbell

A quietly unassuming woman, on meeting her you might not guess that Eileen Campbell is a highly respected Australian and internationally acclaimed artist, author, and tutor. Having worked as a primary school teacher for twenty-two years, she has always had an interest in crafts, including weaving, related textile arts, fabric printing, pottery, bookbinding, calligraphy, and photography. Eileen began her voyage into patchwork and quilting in 1984 and it has been her passion ever since, taking her to places she never dreamed she'd go. However it was not until 1993 that Eileen's true ardor took her career in a new direction and she started working full-time as a textile artist, giving workshops and lectures first in Australia and then internationally.

EILEEN SOON FOUND HER TRUE FORTE was in machine appliqué, embroidery, and quilting techniques – skills at which she excels, in fact it is safe to say she is one of the best in the world at her craft. Her designs usually incorporate flora and fauna, whether from nature or imagination, with her work often being embellished with beads, braids, and trims, adding dimension to her appliqué and magnificent machine quilting.

Winning too many awards in quilt shows and exhibitions around Australia to mention, including numerous best-of-shows, Eileen's name soon became a household word in the Australian quilting world. Her fame then spread beyond Australian shores as her quilts were regularly featured in such Australian publications as *Down Under Quilts* and *Australian Patchwork & Quilting*, which are distributed internationally.

Eileen is the author of three books – *Appliqué Applied* (1994), *U is for Unicorn* (1998; since retitled *Creative Medieval Designs for Appliqué*), and *Ideas for Appliqué – The Appliqué Artist's Workbook* (2008) – and has also made several videos and saleable patterns.

Her spectacular quilts have won awards both in Australia and overseas, with Eileen having had quilts included in 'The Husqvarna Viking International Challenge' – *Feel Free* – and also in their 'Color, Couleur, Colore, Kulor' international challenge. Her Pelican Twilight won Best of World when it was entered in the 'World Quilt and Textile Competition' (USA) in 2002, and *Iris Variations* won Best Machine Workmanship – Innovative section in the 2007 'World Quilt & Textile Contest' (USA).

Eileen was an invited guest artist for the Japanese traveling exhibition 'Contemporary Images in Japanese Quilts' in 2004, and a contributor to the 'Three Countries Challenge' (Japan, Australia, and France) in 2006.

Eileen continues her 'appliqué journey', delighting her grandchildren with her fantasy quilts. Tutoring is one way she feels she can contribute to the industry she loves and to give back a little of what it has so generously given her. Her quilts remain an inspiration to all who view them.

**For more details on Eileen's quilts or lecture tours, you can email her (eileen@herplace.net).**

# BE CRE8IVE –
# DECOR8ING THE 8 WORLD
## *Eileen Campbell*

This is a fantasy piece depicting some events in the cre8ive world of '8'. The little 8 men are busy decor8ing and rushing Bernina packages to the stitching world (with some unexpected hiccups!).

As well as 'serious' quilt designs, Eileen sometimes uses a more zany approach (usually for a grandchild) and she has created a series of action-dragons that can be found skating, abseiling, yachting, and the like.
When Eileen saw the signature Bernina '8', with its asymmetrical shape, she thought at once that with legs and arms the '8' could be transformed into a little person. This '8' person, should we say many of them, could then tell the world to 'Be Cre8ive'. So this is how the '8' people came to be picking flowers to decor8 the letters hanging from the tree, jumping from aeroplanes delivering Bernina machines, or rushing these machines to places on bicycles and skateboards. Of course nothing ever seems to run smoothly, and things happen along the way. There is lots to look out for in this '8-World', including a few more '8' men in the quilting!

BARB CLEAVER
PETRIE, QLD, AUSTRALIA

Barb Cleaver has been married to her childhood sweetheart, Mark, for thirty-six years and has three great sons and two daughters-in-law – Seth, Luke, Lauren, Ben, and Jess. She's a proud 'Nana' of grandson Josh, and grand-daughters Sophie, Ebony, and Charli.

BARB ATTRIBUTES HER TALENT to her very gifted mother, who encouraged her from a young age to work with needle and thread, with both a sewing machine and by hand.

However, it wasn't until 1984 that she really ventured into patchwork and quilting, taking a class in Sydney with Noni Fisher. Her skills and passion quickly grew and by 1987 Barb was teaching appliqué and piecing locally. Then in 1989, realizing the need for a quilt shop in her hometown of Caboolture, Barb joined forces with her friend Hilda Nichols to open Quilters Quarters in the town's main street.

She sold the business in 1990 and has since been a freelance tutor, sharing her skills extensively around Australia. She has also taught in New Zealand and the UK, and more recently for humanitarian projects in Banda Aceh, Indonesia, and Vanuatu.

Barb is best known for her love of Fibonacci – the theory of proportional measurements, which makes choosing the various sizes of the parts of a quilt virtually foolproof. Due to persistent, painful back issues, Barb works chiefly with the 'quilt-as-you-go' method in the construction of quilts. This, along with Fibonacci, forms a large part of her various workshop techniques.

Barb and her work have been featured and profiled in over twenty-five patchwork and quilting publications both in Australia and overseas, but quilting is not the only thing that has given her much joy. She has been guest speaker at various fundraising events, as well as church and community functions.

These days Barb promotes Bernina sewing machines and receives sponsorship from the Bernina Sewing Centre in Chermside. She also works as a tutor for Bernina at quilt and craft shows in southeast Queensland.

When asked where she is heading from here, Barb explains: 'As I look at where my work is going and what really gets me excited, I would have to say that I am traveling more down the road of non-traditional quiltmaking, moving more into the field of textile art using surface embellishments and fiber treatments.' Barb continues to explain what is really her passion for the future: 'But in saying all that, I believe I will always love teaching beginners, encouraging people to start their own creative journey and watching them grow both in spirit and talent – this is the real buzz when it comes to patchwork and quilting for me.'

You can contact Barb via email (barb@barbcleaver.com.au) for more information about her class schedule, or visit her website (www.barbcleaver.com.au) to view her quilts.

barb cleaver

# 8-UNCONTAINABLE CREATIVITY
## *Barb Cleaver*

Barb wanted to craft a piece that depicted the '8' exploding with creativity. As a nature lover, she chose to do this with flowers and butterflies that represent uncontrolled freedom. In keeping with this concept, her '8' needed to be open, and so she chose felting, free-motion embroidery, machine embroidery, and bobbin work, to mention just a few of the machine artistry techniques incorporated in her quilt. In doing so she has represented Bernina machine artistry exploding with uncontainable creativity.

SANDY CORRY
COFFS HARBOUR, NSW, AUSTRALIA

Sandy has always made things, with her earliest memories including putting bits and pieces together to fashion lovely items. As a child, her life was grim, harsh, and impoverished, so being creative helped make her life more tolerable and pleasant. Throughout life, Sandy always tries to find a way to make the most of whatever situation she finds herself in. As such, her life has been a wonderful journey, filled with interesting people who have shared their love of creating, experimenting, learning, and producing beautiful things.

SANDY COMPLETED A COURSE IN DRESSMAKING, pattern drafting, and design in her early twenties, giving her the basics (and more) in sewing, and sparking her interest in sewing and dressmaking.

During the thirty years Sandy lived in the lovely NSW inland town of Inverell, she taught in the Aboriginal community and at the TAFE college, which led her to open up her own sewing school for young people and adults, teaching all aspects of sewing.

It was during this time that Sandy developed an infatuation for quiltmaking, and it was this passion that eventually took over and saw her working exclusively within this field. What an adventure her quilting journey has been!

In 2002 Sandy moved to the idyllic NSW coastal town of Coffs Harbour. It is here that she became totally inspired by the beauty of the constantly changing ocean, the azure coast, the lush rainforest, rivers, and verdant vegetation.

Sandy has won many awards for her quilts, including the 2001 'Dayview Textiles Challenge'. Her work has been extensively published in such prestigious magazines as *Down Under Quilts*, *Australian Patchwork & Quilting*, *Australian Patchwork & Stitching*, and *New Zealand Quilter*, and she was a feature artist in the book *Color Play* by Joen Wolfrom, published by C&T Publishing in the US.

After many years of traveling throughout Australia and New Zealand, teaching quiltmaking, Sandy is now content to stay put and work at her textile art studio. Here she enjoys being creative – 'playing' and experimenting with paints, dyes, and any medium that applies color to fabric to make it appear more enchanting to the eye, whether it be in the form of a bed quilt, wall quilt, or art piece.

To be able to spend her time teaching and sharing her knowledge with like-minded creative artists fills Sandy's days now. Students and artists who live locally or travel from afar and wish to join Sandy in her fabric and thread adventures meet at her studio – The Fabric Art Studio – in the center of Coffs Harbour. Here they delight in fashioning inspirational textile art objects that are and will be treasured museum pieces of the future, carrying Sandy's legacy on for generations to come.

**You can visit Sandy's studio in Coffs Harbour Plaza, or her website (www.sandycorry.com), or drop her an email (corry@northnet.com.au) for more information on her classes and quilts.**

sandy corry

# ULTIM8LY ...
## *Sandy Corry*

This wall-hanging is a compilation of various techniques: traditional, modern, and innovative. Creating this quilt brought Sandy great pleasure as she met the challenges of exploring new techniques. The quilt is made from a cotton sateen canvas with duchess satin used for the decorative border, and printed cotton for the leaf-like feathers, picture shadow, quilt binding, and backing. Cotton and polyester threads are used for the quilting and embellishments, along with Shira oil paint sticks, cotton batting for the quilting, and polyester batting for the trapunto.

SUE DENNIS
SUNNYBANK, QLD, AUSTRALIA

Early memories of seeing her Czechoslovakian grandmother's colorful embroideries, sewing lessons at school, fashion, design, and dressmaking for herself and her young family gave Sue a love of creative sewing. This passion and those lessons remain with her today as she designs and stitches her contemporary art quilts.

SUE BEGAN HER QUILTING CAREER in 1990 while living in the remote mining town of Mt Isa in northwest Queensland. Mt Isa's isolation meant that fabric and books had to be mail-ordered from larger towns and cities; learning techniques such as appliqué and piecing from such a distance also meant that firm quilting friendships were established. Sue started with traditional quilting patterns using bright colors, machine piecing, and machine quilting. She later began teaching workshops in Mt Isa and outlying rural centers, spreading the love of rotary cutter patchwork techniques and machine quilting.

With a transfer to Sardinia, Italy in 1995 for her husband Bob, Sue immersed herself in the artistic side of the Italian life, resulting in her quilt, *La Finestra su Tuili*, which became part of the Cagliari City Permanent Quilt Collection.

On her return to Australia, experimentation and finding her own voice led Sue to favor numerous surface design techniques, free-motion stitching, and bold design that catch the eye and the imagination.

In 2001, Sue's quilt *What Would You Take?* was the winner of 'Australian Quilts in Public Places', and was acquired by the Immigration Museum in Melbourne.

Sue has been awarded many prizes for her distinct, original art quilts and has been invited to exhibit internationally. Her quilts have been shown in juried and group exhibitions throughout Australia, New Zealand, the USA, Great Britain, Europe, South Africa, Taiwan, and the Middle East. She also has a wide publication history that adds to her portfolio.

Other professional quilt-related activities Sue has been or is involved in include being asked to be a judge, juror, and curator at exhibitions. She is the Australian coordinator for the 'World Quilt & Textile' and 'State of Art '09' exhibitions. As a professional artist she is a member of Studio Art Quilt Associates, an SAQA Oceania representative, Chair of 2QAQ (Queensland Quilters Art Quilts), and Quilters' Guild of NSW Inc. She is an accredited teacher in Special Techniques and a member of Quilts International Inc., Queensland Quilters Inc., The Quilters' Guild of NSW Inc., Ozquilt Network Inc., and Sunnybank Quilters.

**For more information on Sue's activities and upcoming events, visit her website (www.suedennis.com) or her blog (www.suedennisartquilts.blogspot.com).**

sue dennis

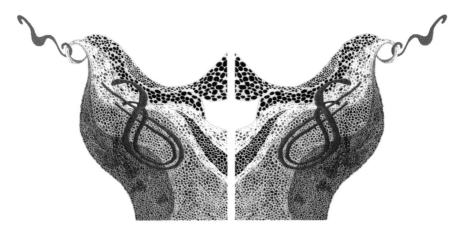

# CAPTIV8ING
## *Sue Dennis*

The new Bernina *8-Series* will captivate Australian sewing enthusiasts and Sue wanted to capture the excitement of the moment by using the structure of a net to capture the red '8'. More than 5,000 meters of metallic thread were stitched onto a soluble stabilizer base to create the net-like fabric that captures the '8'. Free-motion quilting finishes the quilt.

It was an interesting challenge for Sue to work in the limited color palette of black, silver, white, and red. White rayon thread gave parts of the net a softer feel to the purely metallic thread sections.

The canvas for the whole-cloth quilt was a cotton/linen blend with the white and silver 'fabric' being freehand appliquéd onto the canvas. Hobbs *Heirloom Premium 80/20* batting was sandwiched between the quilt top and the commercial cotton quilt silk backing fabric. Silk thread, Madeira metallic and rayon, as well as cotton thread, are used for the freehand embroidery.

Machine freehand thread fabric, appliqué, quilting, and couching are the techniques Sue used in her quilt.

SUSAN FILER
CLEAR ISLAND WATERS, QLD, AUSTRALIA

SUSAN OFTEN COMMENTS that she did not come from a crafty family, however when she looks back she can remember that both her parents were always fixing and mending things, mostly to make them last a little longer – knitting, building, servicing the car, helping with school projects, home maintenance. It was only later that Susan realized this 'can do' attitude and creative approach to life had a profound effect on the way she approached her own life. Why buy mass-produced, she wondered, if you could make an original, creating something from nothing and really enjoying the process.

Susan has always been involved in craft and creative pursuits and cannot recall a time when she did not have an imaginative project in the pipeline – she is always 'pottering' away on some new pursuit. After all these years Susan still can't seem to find the right words to adequately describe the thrill she gets from experimenting with a new artistic technique, and then seeing it unfold in her hands.

Learning to sew on her gran's treadle machine, Susan was over the moon when she moved on to an electric model sewing machine, which her mother had won. Susan progressed from dolls' clothes to her own clothes, and later even her wedding dress and then, in due course, her children's clothes. She even ventured into making her husband's clothes!

With several different projects on the go at any one time, Susan has been inspired to incorporate these diverse aspects in the one project. For example, she will include cross stitch, embroidery (both hand and machine), and ribbon work in the one design, because she loves the life these different textures bring to her projects. Susan's latest projects have three-dimensional aspects, using a multitude of materials such as metal leaf, beads, wire, and sculptural elements.

Although Susan has been crafting most of her life, she is a relative newcomer to quilting. She lived in Hong Kong for several years and when her family moved to Singapore, she joined a quilting class as a way to meet new people and make friends. From the moment she pieced her first nine-patch block she was bitten by the quilting bug and has been stitching quilts ever since. Susan owes a debt of gratitude to her expat friends, who now live all over the world. These people tirelessly answered all her quilting questions, helping her make sense of quilting terminology and the 'rules' (although, having the highest regard for her fellow quilters, Susan is not so sure about the so-called 'quilting rules', and prefers instead the motto: If it works, go with it until you find something better!).

Over the past ten years Susan has had the opportunity to teach in New Zealand, the USA, Hong Kong, Singapore, and Australia. Her work has been widely published in Australian magazines also.

A pivotal skill for Susan was designing and crafting the latest trend jewelry for her friends in high school, which was something she then turned into a small business. Over the years she has run a successful mail-order store, and lately she has been focusing her energies on a pattern publishing company, The Pattern Place.

Now settled on the Gold Coast and with her children in their senior years of high school, Susan is kept busy designing for her business, while at the same time gaining a great deal of pleasure from exhibiting at the major craft shows around Australia. Seeing a gap in the market for truly inspiring yet simple projects, Susan has made it her aim to produce projects that are achievable for beginner stitchers, yet are fun and fresh. Quilters are looking beyond traditional designs and hopefully Susan's patterns have provided an alternative source of inspiration.

As was the case with her quilting classes in Singapore, it is the people Susan meets that have the most profound effect on her as they influence not only her designing but the new techniques and products she experiments with. Crafting has taken Susan on such a fascinating journey, and as we all continually push at the boundaries of stitching, she can only wonder where she will venture next.

**You can contact Susan via email (susan@patternplace.com.au), or visit her website (www.patternplace.com.au) for information on her classes, products, and craft show appearances.**

# THE NEW BERNINA 8
# LETS YOUR CREATIVITY FLY
*Susan Filer*

A soft sculpture in the form of the number 8, to symbolize the '8' on the new Bernina 8-*Series* long arm, sewing, and embroidery machines. This sculpture is designed to showcase and combine built-in machine decorative stitching, techniques from traditional sewing, embroidery, and quilting in an unexpected three-dimensional manner that truly transforms the ordinary number 8 into a cre8ive '8'.

JULIE HADDRICK
BLACKWOOD, SA, AUSTRALIA

julie haddrick

Julie Haddrick is an award-winning contemporary Australian quiltmaker. She specializes in original stained glass and appliqué wall quilts, and her work features hand-dyed and printed fabrics. Julie teaches art-oriented design techniques that encourage originality, confidence, and creative expression in her students. Along with her husband Peter, Julie operates *Haddrick on Fabric* in Blackwood, South Australia, where she designs her stunning wall quilts and patterns.

AS A CHILD JULIE WAS CREATIVE, energetic, untidy, cheeky, and a non-conforming tomboy. Using an antiquated sewing machine, she created anything 'arty' without the use of a pattern (except for her clothing, which of course the creative Julie modified). Julie's early years were full with her teaching schedule, home-making, interior decorating, gardening, stained glass, and renovating old houses – bored was not a word in Julie's vocabulary!

Her fine arts training (where she majored in drawing and painting) and many years employed as a high school teacher of art, craft, and design, have kept Julie within creative contexts. So much of her paid work has been giving out, nurturing, and engendering the creative expression in others. Now, through quilting, the frustration to express herself has finally been addressed.

At a time in her life when she was continually challenged by poor health, Julie read a book called *That Quilt has a Story*, by Robyn Ginns, and was hooked. Immediately she enrolled in Robyn's needleturn appliqué class and the creative doors flew open.

To combat painful hours of ongoing health problems, Julie would draw, carrying a 'weeny' blank book with her everywhere she went. This book provided the focus of distraction from the pain, and rekindled her love of drawing. Following some sketches in the garden, her first stained glass quilt – *Iris in Favrile* – evolved in *1999*. *Lemon in Favrile* followed and was a successful entry in the exhibition 'Australian Bounty'.

Julie's years of part-time study seemed to link with her quilting pursuits. Skills and ideas from leadlight classes overlapped into textiles. Louis Comfort Tiffany, the famed American glass artist and maker of opalescent 'Favrile' glass, was an influence, as was the work of English designer William Morris. Studies in textile dyeing, printing, embellishing, and construction in the 1980s provided the basis for her works today. When purchased quilting fabrics did not provide the diversity of cloth Julie needed, she dyed and printed her own. As her evolving skills as a quilt artist come from fine art rather than a sewing background, this makes her work difficult to slot into the patchworking traditions.

Julie incorporated color, forms, and floral symbolism in her third quilt – *Women in My Studio* – the AQIPP winning entry in 1999 and the first competition she'd entered.

Julie's quilts attracted so much interest she was asked to teach, and her experiences teaching alongside eminent quilters at events like 'Federation Fling' in Perth, 'Quilt Encounter' in Adelaide, the 'NZ Quilt Symposium' in Christchurch, as well as a huge variety of country and interstate workshops, are a privilege for her.

Julie's art is open ended, changing with and responding to the times. Her work now focuses on Australian native flora and birds, and she is drawn to the 'snapshot view'. She enjoys the surprise element of quilting, in her and other's textile art work.

**Contact Julie for her teaching schedule, or view her quilts on her website (www.haddrickonfabric.com.au).**

# CRE8 FOR BERNINA
## *Julie Haddrick*

The Bernina *Ultimate Creative Challenge* was indeed a challenge for Julie as her personal style and artistic genre is quilt-organic and in many ways spiritual. Her current work focuses on the essence of objects, and our connectedness to the universe, of one thing to another; living or non-living and valuing the fact that objects do not exist in isolation. This challenge was for Julie to incorporate a number 8 and use a specific color scheme in the overall design.

In designing *Cre8*, Julie explored ways of depicting 'the creative cycle', from the frustration of an idea to the development and refinement that leads to creative solutions. Earthly colored ribbons represent ideas that intersect as a nest of 8 eggs, clustered in the lower section of the red '8'. Inspirational phrases from the Bernina 830 brochure combine in these ribbons as hand-painted and quilted words in subtle colors. They in turn develop skyward and become waves of delight that appear as splashes of inspiration, releasing the solution – a white dove. As the dove takes flight, the journey of the other birds can be seen in the distance. Inspiration threads its way through the design, represented as a ribbon of lightly beaded, block-printed fabric. The birds take on a life of their own and the circle begins again. The largest white feather symbolizes beyond boundaries; the freedom to be creative and the flight to creative fulfillment. Decorative stitching and beautiful quilting showcase some of the many qualities Julie loves most about her Bernina.

JUDY HOOWORTH
MORISSET, NSW, AUSTRALIA

judy hooworth

Judy is a leading inaugural Australian quilt-maker and artist, having been infatuated with patchwork since 1960. Starting out as an art teacher, Judy studied at the National Art School from 1963 to 1966, and it was after this time that she became fascinated with making patchwork quilts and stitching textiles.

WHILE JUDY HAS ALWAYS LOVED working with traditional quilt designs, she also began to design her own contemporary quilts, and has continued with this double focus, making pieced innovative quilts with a modern twist that result in uniquely designed art quilts.

Judy very soon became renowned for the way she used bold and brilliant color in her quilts, which were being widely exhibited in Australia and around the world. She won the prestigious Quilt National four times, and since 1981 has become a much-in-demand tutor and lecturer, both in Australia and abroad.

Judy's quilts have been widely published in many books and magazines throughout Australia and internationally. She is the instigating founder of Australia's first juried and longest running contemporary quilt exhibition, 'The New Quilt'. She has been involved in the writing and publication of three books: *Razzle*

*Dazzle Quilts*, *Spectacular Scraps*, and *Quilts on the Double* (the latter two were co-authored with her friend Margaret Rolfe). Judy's quilts are also represented in public and private collections in Australia, the UK, and the USA. Her work can be found nationally in the Tamworth City Art Gallery and internationally in the prestigious Museum of Arts and Design, in New York. She was awarded the Quilters' Guild NSW Inc. Study Scholarship in 1994 and a Professional Development Grant that was funded by the Australian Council for Visual Arts/Crafts in 1995.

For the past twenty-five years, Judy has taught and practiced from her studio in Tamworth where she delights in passing on her vast knowledge and experience to eager, like-minded students, and creating new and fascinating works of art.

You can email Judy (judyhooworth@ozemail.com.au) for information on her appearance, and teaching schedule.

# QUADRILLE
## *Judy Hooworth*

For this challenge, Judy rummaged through her fabric stash collecting as many fabrics as she could find that were in the challenge colors of red, black, white, and silver. She discovered a brilliant selection of cotton prints, and after 'living' with them for a while she designed an original quilt using appliquéd blocks split with sashing. The combination of spots, stripes, and prints gave the *Quadrille* quilt a dramatic effect and, from a distance, that wow factor – bright and striking. It certainly makes a statement, just like the *8-Series* machines.

LEAENDA INGRAM
SYLVANIA, NSW, AUSTRALIA

leaenda ingram

Creating and digitizing machine embroidery designs is Leaenda's passion; she is dedicated to style and her designs are inspired by the brilliant works of hand-embroidered garments from around the world.

LIKE MANY MACHINE-ARTIST TUTORS and textile crafters, Leaenda discovered her love of sewing from a very early age with her grandmother's Singer treadle sewing machine. With the recent and rapid advances in technology in the sewing industry, she has kept up with the ever-changing world of digitizing software (both domestic and professional), producing embroidery designs for the fabulous sewing/embroidery machines we know today.

Leaenda is currently Senior Trainer for the Australian College of Computer Embroidery and Textile Technology. She is a qualified trainer and assessor, having gained her Certificate III qualification in digitizing and computerized hoop embroidery. This on-line college is the first in the world to offer such a course to Australian and international students through their on-line learning center.

Leaenda is passing on her considerable embroidery knowledge and digitizing skills in the hope of lifting the standard and level of computerized embroidery in Australia.

She has taught workshops and seminars on embroidery and digitizing throughout Australia and the United States and is committed to furthering the qualifications available to eager students in the embroidery field.

Digitizing led Leaenda to the creation of her own design business – Leaenda's Sewbiz – which was established in 1998 and offers a diversified range of embroidery design collections including stained glass, Shisha mirror, Richelieu faux cutwork, and exquisite white-work embroidery. Leaenda has digitized designs for many Australian companies and her work has been widely published in such prestigious Australian magazines as *Creative Expressions*, *Textile Art and Machine Embroidery*, and *Stitches*.

**You can contact Leaenda via email (Designs@leaendasewbiz.com.au), or visit her website (http://www.leaendasewbiz.com.au) for information on her designs and teaching schedule.**

# TIME PIECE 8
## *Leaenda Ingram*

Feature back neck piece and dress – yes, the dress came after the extravagant *Time piece '8'* neck piece. The supporting dress is made from black and red Lycra jersey fabric with a tulle drop skirt. A black and white feature cord wraps around the body of the black Lycra, edging the red asymmetrical shawl with fringe-like figure 8s as a trim on the shawls cap sleeve. The feature back neck piece of cascading embroidered figure 8s and spiderweb-like threads is suspended by three spaced and matching black and white twisted cords, which are draped around the front of the neck and follow the asymmetrical back neckline.

DEBORAH LOUIE
JANNALI, NSW, AUSTRALIA

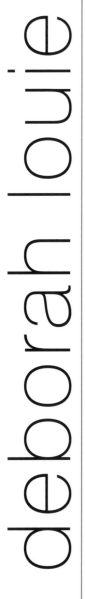

DEBORAH STUDIED TEXTILES, color, and design after leaving school and then worked as a production manager for a textile printing company for a period, enjoying working with fabrics and being part of the fashion industry.

She started quilting when she had her first child, Sam, in 1990, and ever since then Deborah has been passionate about quilting. Like so many quilters, Deborah had to experiment by making every style of quilt imaginable before she decided on her own style. After her second child Claire arrived, and when both her children were in school, Deborah wanted to start working again and so she started quilting at home for friends, using her domestic machine. The word spread with amazing speed and within a few months Deborah had a year's worth of quilting booked in!

Deborah treated each quilt as if it were her own, quilting it with much love and care. Her reward came in the form of the many awards her clients' quilts won at national and regional quilt shows. Her business was based at home for over six years, but then in the year 2000 she decided to share her knowledge with students who were eager to take advantage of her knowledge and skills. Teaching has now become her passion and full-time job as she teaches her students how to quilt the 'Deborah Louie Way'!

Deborah is a Quilters, Guild of NSW Accredited Special Techniques Machine Quilting Teacher. The Quilters, Guild of NSW has twice awarded her with Excellence in Domestic Machine Quilting, and she was awarded First Prize in Domestic Machine Quilting twice in the Darling Harbour Quilt and Craft show, held annually in Sydney – a great thrill. Australian quilting magazines have featured Deborah's work extensively also.

Quilting has afforded so many wonderful opportunities to Deborah, including beautiful friends and the chance to travel and teach wonderful quilters. As a passionate quilting teacher, her conviction is that a student gets a great deal of satisfaction and pride when she has completed the quilting of a quilt. Deborah teaches domestic machine quilting nationally, teaching six levels of machine quilting as well as machine appliqué.

Deborah incorporates a holistic approach in her teaching, where all avenues are addressed to give the students the skills they require to gain the confidence and ability to quilt. Each student's needs are unique and Deborah endeavors to give each individual the time and caring commitment they need to be successful.

Deborah's reward comes when her students realize that they have mastered new skills and are empowered with the knowledge that they can make beautiful quilts from start to finish. Students soon become confident and come to the realization that machine quilting is not just an afterthought but rather it completes and enhances a quilt. Machine quilting is a very desirable skill, as the more one quilts the more confident one becomes.

Students start out with the 'Let's Quilt' two-day class where they learn how to prepare a quilt for quilting using Deborah's unique pinning technique – this ensures they never get puckers on the quilt backing fabric. They go on to explore threads, needles, machine tension, stitch length, beautiful neat stopping and starting, perfect ditching, the lift and drag technique, the correct use of a walking foot, cross hatching, cables, and the all-important theory of how and where to start quilting with efficient turning of the quilt under the sewing machine. Students can then advance to free-motion quilting, machine trapunto (to add maximum lift and texture to their quilting), and even commercial stencil-line quilting which is great for borders, sashes, and blocks. Then there is echo quilting, twin-needle quilting, bobbin quilting, metallic thread quilting, keyline quilting, continuous one-line quilting (where color and shading are added to the quilting) – the list is endless and Deborah is a master of them all.

Quilting on a Bernina makes machine quilting very efficient, allowing the quilter to achieve great results every time. The walking foot feeds a heavy quilt beautifully when 'ditch' stitching, and Deborah prefers to 'ditch' stitch all her piecing first as it makes the quilt strong and flat. It also allows the piecing to sit beautifully, making it easy to then add free-motion and other styles of quilting to enhance and decorate the quilt.

Deborah's favorite technique is a feathered keyline trapunto technique, as this gives such a classic timeless elegance to a quilt. She enjoys making traditional and contemporary quilts, but to Deborah all quilts are beautiful because they come from the heart, and she feels very blessed to be able to work with her passion.

You can contact Deborah via email (deborahlouie@optusnet.com.au) or visit her website (www.deborahlouie@internode.com.au) for details on her classes and teaching schedule.

# FEATHERED FLORAL MEDLEY
## *Deborah Louie*

Deborah's quilt is in three parts, and explores the many techniques that she loves to use. She designed the border '8' design to repeat around the left border and top of the quilt, to represent the elegant shape of the new 830 series. Deborah then trapuntoed the shapes and quilted them using a black keyline. A multi-echo swirl has been added in the background as a dense filler to lift the trapunto, with soft shading to add color.

The center design is free-motion appliqué, using elegant back floral shapes inspired by an Italian flocked fabric with a small red keyline to represent the Bernina challenge colors of black, white, red, and silver, with echo-quilting around the shapes.
The right side of the quilt represents the freedom one can have on a much larger quilting area on the *8-Series* Bernina machines, with quilters being free to explore patterns and shapes without feeling restricted. Deborah stitched the floral shapes first in silver thread and she then added a black keyline. Finally she shaded her work with soft color. This gave a modern free-form pattern to match the modern style of the new Bernina *8-Series* machines.

JEN LUCK
HIGHFIELDS, QLD, AUSTRALIA

Jen lived for many years with her husband on a grain farm near the Darling Downs, around three hours west of Brisbane. She has recently retired to Highfields, near Toowoomba in Queensland.

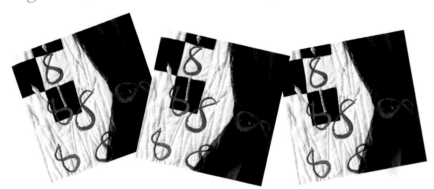

STITCHERY, whether by machine or by hand, has always been Jen's passion. From a very young age she remembers helping her mother manage their large family by assisting in making everything the family wore.

Her first Bernina was purchased in 1954, from a Mr Roberts of Brisbane – it was instead of a dinner set for her 'hope chest' in preparation for her marriage! While in the store, Jen met a free-motion embroiderer who taught her the skill of freehand embroidery. This lady stitched the most beautiful roses and other flowers, literally drawing with a sewing machine needle. Whenever Jen went to the city, this lady would teach her how to practice drawing with just with a sewing machine needle. Then, as Jen's family grew, she continued to study all aspects of textile art including fabric painting, dying (there was no access to printed fabrics at this time), and sewing.

Soon Jen was proficient in all forms of embroidery and she began her work as a teacher. Over the last twenty years she has taught quilting for TAFE, the Queensland Arts Council, and the Australian Quilters. Not limiting her fame in her own backyard, in 1992 she was also invited to be a tutor at the International Pacific Festival in San Francisco, USA.

In addition to having taught textiles and been a qualified tailoress and dressmaker, Jen completed training in hand-finishing garments. Not only is she a proficient tailoress, she also taught decorative fashion for the Southern Queensland Institute of TAFE for ten years. Now, after her involvement in the field of textiles for the last thirty years, Jen has explored a variety of textile art techniques and quilting is just one of them! Initially she worked mostly with creative appliqué and machine embroidery, but she then moved into applying these techniques in her quilts.

Jen's passion for textiles in all forms creates the challenges she faces when she is designing a piece and then transferring a concept onto fabric, as was the case when she was interpreting her impressions of summer in Western Australia into a quilt form. Aptly named *Dreaming of the Kimberleys*, this quilt featured in the Australian magazine *Patchwork & Quilting*. Jen chose to use a wide variety of techniques to create her sensations of the bright light and plant forms of Australia's far west.

Jen enjoys traveling in the remote bushland areas of Australia, sharing her knowledge with other country women and enabling them to use their skills so they can support themselves and even market their art in local galleries for the tourist trade. This is one way these women can express what they see and make a garment with flair. Teaching her craft and passing on her passion to eager students was always Jen's first love, but it was often overtaken by the necessity of work on the farm. Fortunately she had a very supportive husband who encouraged her to continue teaching whenever she could.

Bernina has always supported Jen when she has traveled and taught, allowing the use of their machines in classes, sponsoring and supporting shows, exhibitions, and conventions. Bernina keeps their 'friends' up-to-date with all their new products, which in turn keeps us abreast of new technology and exciting advances in the sewing, quilting, and textile industry. Jen is very appreciative of this and thanks Bernina Australia.

You can contact Jen via email (jenl@westnet.com.au) for information on her teaching schedule.

# HIGH EXPECTATIONS
## *Jen Luck*

Keeping in mind the color scheme chosen by Bernina Australia to promote the new Bernina *8-Series* machines, Jen also decided to use some of the machine's many features. *High Expectations* was pieced with the 1/4in patchwork foot using a lettering font chosen from the design software, and then embroidered. As she had to draw the special '8' feature, she decided to digitize it on the Bernina software in various sizes, and then use these as part of the foliage and curtain holder which are freeform. Keeping the checkered rows straight as she pieced the face over a padded area was quite a challenge. Using bleach on the black cotton fabric, Jen produced marks representing moonlight, which she defined with touches of gold stitching. The rose was made using hand-dyed fabric which was applied by hand. The hair was then hand-embroidered, adding another dimension.

In today's world we often hide behind a mask in our relationships with others as we travel on our life's journey. The inspiration for Jen's quilt came from a poem that speaks about hiding behind a mask to cover our feelings when things don't work out. The emotional theme of the quilt represents Jen's observations of the struggle to find that special 'one' to share your life with, be it through dating, personal ads, or just a chance meeting.

DENISE MAY
BRISBANE, QLD, AUSTRALIA

denise may

Denise May has been using needles all her life. From the age of five she was learning to knit using five-inch nails and darning wool, and then she progressed on to skewers from the local butcher!

ALWAYS OBSESSED when it came to being creative, Denise experimented with all forms of stitching: dressmaking, crochet, knitting, cross stitch, and sewing, all on her Bernina machines and Baby Lock serger/overlocker. She always had some form of needlework in her hands.

Upon retiring in the early 1990s, Denise discovered patchwork and her quilts then multiplied like wire coathangers in a wardrobe! *Cathedral Windows* and *Wedding Ring* quilts are two of her favorite patchwork designs.

When the Bernina 180 embroidery machine came into Denise's life it opened up a whole new world – that of machine embroidery. This in turn created a new learning curve for Denise as she enrolled in classes at Bernina Chermside. In one of these classes she made the Latte quilt, designed by Kerrie Hay, and chose shades of soft pink to make it with. Attending these classes inspired Denise and her quest for knowledge became insatiable.

It was her passion for machine artistry that prompted Denise to enter the Ronald McDonald Challenge through the *Creative Expressions* magazine. The opportunity to produce a block for this worthwhile charity touched Denise's heart, so instead of making one block she made twenty (which were later made into two quilts and then auctioned, with all proceeds going to Ronald McDonald House). Denise did all this work on her Bernina 180 using the Jenny Haskins' Rose design, specifically designed for the challenge.

Denise won the challenge and was awarded a Bernina *440* embroidery machine and design software. This machine has never stopped stitching – not a day goes by when it is allowed to sit idle.

Since then Denise has entered a number of charity competitions, geared to raise money for a worthy cause (which always give, her another excuse to purchase more fabric, batting, threads, and designs!).

Then in 2007, Early May Enterprises Pty Ltd was founded by Denise, her husband David, and their daughter. It is a family-owned company located in Brisbane, Australia, specializing in creating beautiful embroidery designs for children of all ages. EME's aim is to produce high-quality machine embroidery designs using original artworks, especially for the home sewer, worldwide.

It is with delight that Denise makes all the quilts to showcase her stunning designs, which she displays at craft shows throughout Australia. Denise is now also giving classes at these shows, teaching her easy quilt-as-you-go techniques and machine embroidery.

Denise was honored to be asked to participate in the *Bernina Australasian Creative Challenge* to launch the Bernina *8-Series* machines, and accepted with enthusiasm.

**Email Denise (denise@emee.com.au) or visit her website (www.emee.com.au) for more information on her products.**

# 8 DAYS A WEEK
## *Denise May*

Denise designed this soft and cool voile blouse which is perfect to wear in the hot and humid climate of Brisbane, where she lives. *8 Days a Week* represents Denise's wish for at least eight days a week, so that her Bernina 830 could be forever stitching cre8ively, celebr8ing her passion for machine artistry.

VAL MOORE
CHELTENHAM, NSW, AUSTRALIA

Val is one of Australia's founding quilt artists, and one of its most highly respected, having been quilting for over thirty years. For many years she ran a quilting, patchwork, and hand embroidery shop and studio in Pennant Hills; it opened in 1981 and was one of the first of its kind in Sydney.

FLOWERS HAVE ALWAYS HELD A FASCINATION for Val and they have always been a focal point of her quilts. Initially she represented them with exquisite precise pieced appliqué, which she did by hand, but later she developed her amazing machine appliqué techniques. Color is also one of Val's fields of expertise and her use of color attracts and draws viewers into her stunningly executed quilts. Comments such as 'What a beautiful quilt – ah, it's Val Moore – of course, what else would you expect?' are often heard at quilt shows where her quilts are exhibited.

Teaching has always been part of Val's life, from when she first started out in her store and then when she ventured further afield as news of her teaching skills and sensational classes spread. She now teaches various aspects of quilting in locations throughout suburban and country Australia, specializing in hand and machine appliqué techniques in which she is exceptionally skilled. Val's techniques, skills, and magnificent use of color are hallmarks of her quilting artistry. She is proud of the fact that over the past ten years her students' quilts have won numerous awards at each of the prestigious Quilt and Craft shows held annually at Darling Harbour in Sydney.

Val's classes on how to create and develop an idea to make a quilt are based mainly on floral themes – her quilts and classes reflect her fascination in botanical art. This led Val to create patterns and kits, as quilters desired to achieve the same expert use of color and design she had achieved. She currently teaches face-to-face classes and workshops throughout Australia, with her latest addition to her teaching program being an online WebCam teaching program.

Her favorite quilting piece is the *Australian Wildflower* quilt, which is featured on her website. Val would like to invite you to take a few moments to view the individual blocks in detail, as well as her other quilts that are displayed on her Gallery page. Patterns for each block are available to order through her website.

**Visit Val's website (www.simplyval.net) to view her quilts and purchase her products; you will also find continual updates on new concepts (they come as fast as her imagination and Bernina sewing machine can produce them).**

val moore

# MOON FLOWERS
*Val Moore*

Val's first thought when approached to create a piece for the *Bernina Australasian Creative Challenge* to launch their *8-Series* machines was 'How fantastic!'

As flowers are a recurring design feature in Val's appliqué quilts, as well as in her sketches and watercolor paintings, it was to be expected that the embryo for Val's inspiration was fantasy flowers which then materialized into her *Moon Flowers*, bursting forth from the central focal point of the stylistic number 8.

This pillow represented Val's passion for appliqué flowers and her anticipation of the creative opportunities with the new Bernina *8-Series* machines, as her *Moon Flowers* burst into life from the figure '8'.

RUTH OSBORN
SARINA, QLD, AUSTRALIA

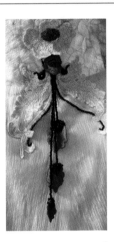

Ruth is a very quiet and modest woman when it comes to her creative ability and artistic flare. Entranced by the beauty of nature and the limitless, amazing source of inspiration it offers for her creations, she is forever taking photographs of flowers, leaves, and the ever-changing colors of the seasons. Ruth has a vast library with a growing array of reference material – it seems the closer she gets to a subject the more incredible it becomes.

WORKING FROM NATURE (which, after all, was created by the Master Designer), Ruth never fails to find endless insight into every facet of color and design – the intricacy of sand patterns, exposed roots of the strangler fig, rainforests, sweet-scented flower beds, and coral reefs – and she endeavors to transfer this inspiration onto fabric, giving it life with dye, thread, and beads.

From sewing through necessity for her children, and then moving on through leatherwork, spinning, and weaving, Ruth's creative journey finally led her to the creative art of machine embroidery. Machine art has so many aspects to explore, and this is the creative road Ruth has chosen, one that has captured her imagination for years and led her to the field of wearable art. That, along with beading, has become Ruth's niche.

Over the years Ruth's wearable art career has had some memorable highlights. She has won numerous awards, been exhibited nationally and internationally, and her work is a treasured possession in many art collections. Ruth has won such awards as The Supreme Award of the Evening, with her gown *Akira Isogowra* (named after Ruth's home-grown personal rainforest). On her success, the following was said of Ruth's gown: 'The divine garment (referring to *Akira Isogowra*) that won was outstanding and should be in a museum because it's beyond fashion.'

Ruth has also won The Supreme Award at 'TAWFA', the 'Harvest Valley National Fashion Awards', the 'FEPA Qld Fashion Awards', and the 'Australian Fashion Network'; she also won The Acquisition Award at 'Fashion Fantasia'.

These days Ruth no longer travels distances to tutor, as she prefers to concentrate on writing articles for our Australian magazines, and working toward exhibitions.

For the future, Ruth sees herself continuing on her creative machine embroidery journey – there is always a new color combination around the next bend in the road, an exciting thread collection, beautiful hand-dyed silks, wools to manipulate, and beads that allure, all of which contribute to Ruth's infinite inspiration. Her greatest inspiration, however, comes from the glory of the natural world that surrounds her.

**Contact Ruth via email (osbornruth1@bigpond.com).**

# DREAM WEAVER
## *Ruth Osborn*

*Dream Weaver* was created specifically for the *'Friends of Bernina Artisan'* competition. Ruth wanted to create something dramatic and feminine, which also typified her classic wearable-art style. The fabric chosen was metallic crinkle cream silk, with a white silk lining. The dress has a strapless pin-tucked and fitted long-line bodice, outlined with lavish embroidery, beading, and sculpted roses, with a flared skirt attached to the bottom of the shaped bodice. The theatrical jacket has a swing back, fluted peplum, fitted sleeves, and a feature collar that encircles a plunging neckline and stands up at the back to reveal a stunning beaded embroidered facet.

81

Ruth used around 10,000 meters of
Madeira silver metallic thread
for the leaves and flowers,
with red and black rayon
as supporting colors.
Using Jenny Haskins'
beautiful embroidery
designs, Ruth then
embroidered
these designs
on black
crystal organza
and *Dissolve
Magic* fiber-
based soluble
stabilizer, with
metallic thread
in the needle
and bobbin, so that
the embroidered flowers
and leaves could be used
as the 'stand-alone' three-
dimensional designs her gown
required. The bodice was machine
embroidered with silver metallic
thread, while the skirt's yoke was
pin-tucked with the same thread Ruth
used for the red embroidered flowers.
Red silk fabric sculpted roses were
added in and among the embroidery to
give added dimension to Ruth's gown.

The embellished area of the gown was then heavily beaded with black jet beading to add depth. The lower edge of the gown has the added embellishment of approximately 1,200 Hot-Fix Crystals, giving a liberal sprinkling of sparkle and a flash of luminosity as the skirt appears to float as the folds move. Ruth suggests one could say she was 'machine dreaming' while creating her *Dream Weaver* gown!

CAROLINE PRICE
MUDGEE, NSW, AUSTRALIA

Caroline and her husband John live on a property at Pyramul (near Mudgee) in the central west of New South Wales. Together they have five adult children who have all flown the nest, but have given them the precious gift of grandchildren. Caroline has been quilting seriously for fifteen years or so. After selling her fabric shop in Bathurst in 1994 (where she also sold Bernina sewing machines), Caroline was diagnosed with breast cancer and, as it has done for many others, quilting became a form of therapy. Quilting was such an addictive pastime that it soon became Caroline's full-time occupation.

MANY OF CAROLINE'S QUILTS have been published with their complete instructions in Australian patchwork and quilting magazines, so that quilters all over Australia have the opportunity to replicate Caroline's techniques and quilts. She has written three books: two on machine appliqué and another on both piecing and machine appliqué, which were co-written with her good friend Michelle Marvig. Her latest book, *Love to Machine Appliqué*, is out now.

Caroline is a well-known and respected quilt tutor who lectures and teaches workshops around Australia and also in New Zealand. Along with Michelle, she also demonstrated and lectured at the IQA Market in Houston, USA. Known mostly as a tutor of machine appliqué, Caroline also teaches other quilting techniques, all of which are done on her beloved Bernina machine. (Caroline has an 'allergy' to hand-sewing needles!)

*Tropical Sunset* is one in a series of Caroline's quilts titled *Landscape Illusions*; other quilts in the collection reflect the countryside of the top end of Australia, where she spent considerable time visiting a daughter who lived in the city of Darwin. Caroline really thinks she was born in the wrong state of Australia, as she adores the glorious Northern Territory with its casual lifestyle, sensational climate, and amazing flora and fauna!

Today Caroline's mission in life is to encourage quilting students by guiding them through new techniques. She wants to inspire them so that they have the confidence to develop their own designs and quilts. Caroline's greatest joy, however, comes from the many friends (both in Australia and overseas) she has made as she has traveled her quilting journey.

**You can email Caroline (price@activ8.net.au) for information on her teaching schedule, books, and products.**

# THE MAGIC WISHING TREE – A FAIRY TALE
## *Caroline Price*

Caroline used many machine stitching techniques in her quilt, showcasing her versatility as a machine artist and how easy it is to become an expert using a Bernina machine. Techniques involving satin, blanket, invisible blind hem, and raw-edge stitching, along with appliqué, free-motion stitching, and quilting, are all featured in her quilt *The Magic Wishing Tree – A Fairy Tale*.

JAN SCHOOTS
CURL CURL, NSW, AUSTRALIA

When she first bought an embroidery machine, Jan's husband Tom was so involved in her obsession for machine embroidery designs that he continually surfed the internet for free designs. As he is Dutch, Tom was fluent in European languages and so he found it easy to translate information found on the Bernina Switzerland site for Jan and was able to keep her abreast of all the latest information.

JAN'S LOVE OF EMBROIDERY AND QUILTING soon led her into the field of teaching, which then became her passion. She loved to first learn exciting new and different techniques for machine embroidery, quilting, software, and overlocking, and then to be able to impart this knowledge to her eager students. She admits to having something of a 'foot fetish', delighting in the various machine feet as they are released and learning new techniques to use them, pushing her machine to the max. She knows that it is only when you do this that new and exciting concepts develop.

For over six years Jan has been in charge of running and coordinating the Sewing Club for Northside Sewing Centre, situated at Narrabeen, a seaside suburb of Sydney. Her classes cover all aspects of the design software, machine embroidery, overlocking, and quilting – a particularly comprehensive class schedule.

Being an avid collector of machine embroidery, textile, overlocking, and quilting magazines, Jan devours their contents and can't wait to try out the projects, always delighting in giving them a 'my version' twist. From these magazines she can keep up with local and international trends, along with sourcing extensive information from the internet. Jan is a firm believer in the fact that we can always learn something new from another tutor; it is then her mission to pass this information on, somewhat like ripples on a pond.

Jan has had regular articles published in the Australian magazines *Machine Embroidery and Textile Art*, and *Stitches*.

In 2007 Jan was awarded the Standard of Excellence (which encompassed all categories), two First places for quilting and a Highly Commended at the Sydney Royal Easter Agricultural Show, which is held annually at Homebush Bay (home of the 2000 Sydney Olympics) for her machine embroidered quilt.

Jan prides herself that she is a member of the NSW Quilters, Guild and has her quilts exhibited with them annually at the Craft and Quilt show, held in Sydney at Darling Harbour.

Tom has sadly been unwell for some time now and as a thank you for all the love and care Jan has bestowed on him during his illness he presented her with a brand new Bernina *830*. Jan cannot wait to put her machine through its paces and push it to its limits!

You can email Jan (curlcurl@primusonline.com.au) for information on her class schedule.

jan schoots

# MACHINE COVER UP
## *Jan Schoots*

*Jan's Machine Cover Up* is a stylish and fitting piece to 'cover up' her new Ultim8. She made it using guesswork (as the new machine had not been released at the time) from quilted silk dupione, and it features embroidered lettering from the Bernina *Embroidery Software V5* as well as techniques from the many fancy feet. Jan is rightly thrilled that the 'cover up' fits her *Ultim8* perfectly, and justly represents its class and style.

CAROLINE SHARKEY
URUNDA, NSW, AUSTRALIA

For the past ten years Caroline, who is fast becoming a well-known figure in the textile art scene in Australia, has had her dream of creating a business doing what she loves (sewing) fulfilled!

RAISING THE PROFILE OF TEXTILE ART and quilting is Caroline's mission in life as she travels extensively, exhibiting, teaching, and bringing attention to her artworks and quilts. She has been an invited judge at the prestigious 'Sydney Quilt Show', is an award-winning quilter, and has had many solo exhibitions at galleries throughout New South Wales as well as around Australia.

As a regular Artist in Residence with Ayers Rock Resort at Uluru (the red center of Australia) over the past eight years, and regularly exhibiting and selling her art at the Uluru Cultural Centre and in Alice Springs, Caroline is particularly well-known in the Australian outback region.

She has been able to develop her skills with the income she receives from the sale of her textile artwork; the interaction she has with clients has resulted in Caroline's art becoming collectors' pieces that are procured by overseas visitors and Australian residents alike.

In her capacity as a tutor, Caroline especially enjoys the time she gets to spend with her students in workshops, relishing the idea that she can inspire them to step outside their comfort zone. She says it is one of the most rewarding aspects of teaching. The time at the end of each class is particularly fascinating for Caroline, for it is at this time that the students (and their teacher) view the results of the class – it is food for Caroline's (and her students') souls.

Many friendships have been made through her classes and Caroline is always in awe of the creativity of the women she comes into contact with, particularly when she hears their life stories and experiences. In 2010 Caroline will be teaching in Fiji and demonstrating at the Bernina stand at the 'New Zealand Symposium', held in Wellington.

One of the highlights of Caroline's career was becoming a 'Bernina Friend' in 2000. The support and friendship she has received from the crew at Bernina is very special. The fact that she had been sewing on a Bernina sewing machine for many years before that made for a very solid business relationship.

Caroline uses fabric and threads as her medium instead of paper and paint, and a sewing machine instead of a brush. The texture, color, and prints of the fabrics she throws together with threads are always fascinating, and often give her inspiration for a new quilt design. Seldom does she draw a quilt design – she instead prefers to let the fabrics, threads, and textures determine her next design on their own. While working toward an idea, Caroline tries to avoid any definite image of the completed piece, because the fabric often reveals surprises that give her unexpected changes of direction in a piece, resulting in exciting results.

Most of Caroline's designs are influenced by her love of the Australian landscape, its unique animals, flora, and reef fish. She is constantly driven by color, striving to find that special 'wow' factor combination. This is Caroline's focus and inspiration and this is what keeps us all waiting to see where it will lead her to next.

**You can view more of Caroline's quilts on her website (www.carolinesharkey.com).**

# 8 POPPIES FOR BERNINA
## *Caroline Sharkey*

The quilt *8 Poppies for Bernina* was designed around the colors of the challenge, with Caroline wanting to showcase the impact of the designated color palette: red, black, silver, and white. The fabrics used in the quilt are made with a technique Caroline uses whereby she slashes, chops, and tears fabric and then stitches it back together again to create a new surface and texture, which is then cut into design shapes and machine embroidered onto the surface of a picture. Caroline added the Bernina ribbon at the lower edge of her quilt to signify her connection with this sewing machine, and the '8' to represent the launching of Bernina *8-Series* sewing technology.

LESSA SIEGELE
ADELAIDE, SA, AUSTRALIA

Lessa is a highly respected and well-known quilt artist and one of the founding members of quilting in Australia, having been actively involved in the Quilters' Guild of South Australia since its inception in 1984. She is a quiltmaker, artist, tutor, and judge, and she is constantly on the road as she teaches and exhibits across the country.

LESSA'S QUILTS HAVE BEEN EXHIBITED in Australia, New Zealand, and the USA, exhibitions where she also finds herself teaching. Her specialty is traditional machine pieced quilts, and it is teaching these techniques that most interests her. Passing on her vast knowledge and experience to avid quilters from beginners to advanced is what brings Lessa most joy as everyone learns something special from her. The delight of seeing others develop a love of quilting as she demonstrates her techniques to achieve accurate piecing is a source of great reward. Lessa aims to create stress-free, fun, entertaining, and informative workshops, while her students learn something new about quilting.

In 2002 Lessa was honored for her services as a tutor in the art of quiltmaking and her contribution to the community through fundraising – she was awarded the OAM (Order of Australia Medal) in the Australian Queen's Birthday Honours. This was an amazing accolade and validation for a woman who has devoted so many years to spreading the 'quilting gospel'.

Lessa was further honored in 2007, by the quilting community this time, when she received the Rajah Award at the 'Australian Quilt Convention' (held annually in Melbourne) for her Outstanding Contribution to Australian Quilting.

So many well-known and accomplished quilters of today owe their start to Lessa – she has been directly responsible for sparking their passion for quilting and for this the sewing and quilting industry owes her an eternal debt of gratitude and admiration.

**You can contact Lessa via email (siegele@internode. on.net) for more information on her class schedules.**

# BERNINA 8 SPINNING AROUND THE WORLD
## *LESSA SIEGELE*

*Bernina '8' Spinning Around the World* is machine pieced and quilted using cotton fabrics and batting. *Around the World* is a traditional pattern (from a very traditional teacher) with the 8s centered on a pivotal axis as if they were spinning – this represents the new Bernina traveling around the quilting world.

CATHY SOTIRIOU
MT GRAVATT, QLD, AUSTRALIA

Textiles have been a substantial part of Cathy's life in one form or another for as long as she can remember. Thinking back to her early childhood, she recalls the joy she found in creating dolls' clothes, something that soon led her to explore hand embroidery.

EVEN WHILE CATHY was studying science (at the same time as she was working for her degree in pathology), her passion for textiles remained alive.

In 1983 Cathy received her first sewing machine, a gift from her husband. It was the trigger to finding her new path in life. She went on to study patternmaking, dressmaking, three-dimensional appliqué, and 'art in design' at the Mackay (north Queensland) TAFE, graduating with honors.

Cathy's fixation with and love of exquisite lace, along with machine and hand embroidery, led her into the romantic world of heirloom sewing. In 1996 she ventured into the creative world of heirloom christening gowns, creating amazingly extravagant gowns (each taking hundreds of hours to make). Such heirloom techniques as intricate insertion and shaped lace, entredeux, pin tucks (straight and curved), puffing, hem stitching using a wing needle, and elaborate hand and machine embroidery were included in each gown. Soon Cathy was being commissioned to make these gowns and a cottage industry sprang up under the label Wiggly Giggly™.

Cathy likes nothing more than to explore her creative side using all the knowledge and techniques she has acquired over the years. She does not plan her projects; rather she enjoys the artistic journey of not knowing what any article or garment she commences will look like until it is finished. Her works of art simply evolve with one technique, piece of lace, or embroidery leading to the next. Her motto: 'Try everything at least once.'

Cathy's beautiful chirstening gowns and heirloom garments, along with step-by-step techniques, have been featured in the Australian dressmaking magazine *Stitches* on many occasions and she runs classes and workshops specializing in heirloom sewing, sewing for beginners, and hand embroidery. Her students' work is a testament to her skills both as an artist and a teacher, and with that motto, who knows what she will try or come up with next?

**Contact Cathy via email (cathysotiriou@gmail.com) for more information on her classes.**

# THE WORKINGS OF A CREATIVE MIND
*Cathy Sotiriou*

This imaginative piece represents the inner workings of a creative person's mind. The mind is constantly moving, jumping from thought to thought and never really resting. The fibers with beads symbolize the actual thought, and the thread/fabric in between is the media required to bring that thought to life. The loose fibers in the tassel are all the ideas that did not work out. The chained '8' is the moment the mind is locked, refusing any further creative thoughts. The piece is not perfect, beautiful, polished, or symmetrical; in fact it appears awkward and uncomfortable. But this is because our minds are not perfect in their creative thought processes; rather they evolve just as the artist does.

KIRRY TOOSE
COWAN, NSW, AUSTRALIA

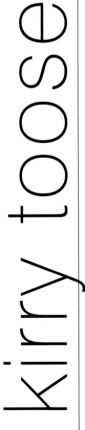

Kirry is an internationally recognized fiber artist extraordinaire who has been a 'Bernina Friend' for more than two decades. Her works are regularly exhibited in regional, private, and community galleries, the Australian Image Gallery, and the 'Art-to-Wear' annual exhibitions held in Sydney, Melbourne, and Perth. She has also had her work exhibited in the prestigious Alexandra Palace in London, along with the 'Fiber Artists' exhibits held in Pittsburgh (USA) and elsewhere around the world.

AFTER COMPLETING a three-year course in dress design at the renowned East Sydney Technical Collage, Kirry followed on with a very traditional career in the 'rag trade' fashion industry.

Now, however, teaching and demonstrating are Kirry's main focus. She is passionately driven by her belief in the validity of the textile arts, and wants to pass on her vast knowledge to the next generation of fiber artists. As well as teaching internationally, Kirry can be seen at all the major shows and exhibitions around Australia, and at private classes and exhibitions in her studio. Her work is widely published in numerous Australian fiber art and embroidery magazines, such as *Creative Expressions*, *Australian Country Craft*, *Stitches*, and *Textile Art and Machine Embroidery*.

Recently Kirry was accepted in the 'World of Wearables' exhibition in New Zealand. She was also a Supreme Award Winner at both 'Fashion Fantasia' and 'Fashion Flair and Fantasy'. Fortunately her artwear has an international appeal – many of her works have been acquired by galleries and private collectors.

Kirry constantly challenges herself by creating innovative art pieces, as her greatest fear is stagnation. Her work practices center on this concept of 'fear and challenge', and her art evolves as a result.

Whether focusing on streamlining a new technique or product, or extending a concept further, Kirry refuses to stand still. Research becomes a multi-leveled factor in her pre-design period, with traditional design elements coming intuitively. The successful combination of these traditional skills (for example hand embroidery), paint, and technology become part of Kirry's current strategies in her art-to-wear concepts and designs.

Kirry can be seen at all major craft, quilting, and wearable art exhibitions and shows around Australia, and is often seen demonstrating at the Bernina stand using her much loved Bernina sewing machine.

**You can email Kirry via email (kirrytoosedesigns@yahoo.com.au) for more information on her teaching schedule and upcoming appearances.**

# ROSES OF 8
## *Kirry Toose*

Created to celebrate the launch of the Bernina *8-Series* embroidery/ sewing machines, the *Roses of 8* ensemble consists of a jacket, dress, and underskirt, constructed with a combination of silk, synthetic, and tulle fabrics. Kirry's personal design brief was to create a fashion garment that was innovative in its use of the figure 8, coupled with digitizing that would reflect her personality and yet appeal to the younger market (a very neglected area in the Art-to-Wear arena). Many of the 'wearable art' garments are not fashion-based and are aimed at the mature woman.

Using the figure '8' as her inspiration in the design concept, Kirry constructed a complicated one-piece, asymmetrical pattern. The difficulty in creating this '8' pattern shape was Kirry's need for the fabric to be able to twist and be shaped into the waist and bodice for exact fitting, and yet not have any waist seam. The sections were individually lined, clipped, turned through, tacked and pressed, and then put together in such a way that they matched at the waist line, and finally they were stitched in place. The simplicity of the dress belies how many days were put into its construction. The striped underskirt was designed and constructed three times to achieve the final balance with the panels. The next self-imposed design area was creating a digitized motif that complemented the outfit, yet had Kirry's personal touch in it, hence the intertwined rose leaf motive in old silver, stitched onto a short abstract jacket with petite puff sleeves. Finally, the collar formed the rose, a complex overlay of pleated fabric forming the petals.

BEV UNWIN
BRISBANE, QLD, AUSTRALIA

Bev is the master of free-motion machine embroidery. Maybe this stemmed from the fact that as a seven-year-old she made her first garment using her mother's electric sewing machine. As she was not allowed to use the 'electricity' part of the machine, she would sit for hours, hand-turning the fly-wheel until her garment was finished. Her joy was complete when she tried the garment on and pranced around her home, much to her parents' amusement and delight.

SO BEGAN BEV'S love affair with sewing machines.

Bev's embroidery journey really started when she purchased her first sewing machine, the result of a promise she made to her dearly beloved and departed grandmother. Bev traded in her grandmother's old treadle machine in order to purchase a brand new shiny black Singer treadle, mounted into a polished timber bench (which she now regrets not keeping).

In her late teens, when Bev was purchasing a new top-of-the-range sewing machine, she encountered an elderly lady sitting at an old treadle sewing machine and creating the most beautiful embroidery. The lady was stitching by moving the fabric (in a hoop) under the needle with such skill and speed it was mesmerizing. Bev does not remember how long she watched, but she was hooked. She left the store knowing that one day she would try to create embroidery as beautiful as that lady had done.

Sewing came easily to Bev; reading and following pattern directions and then constructing a garment was not only a real joy and pleasure, but cost-saving as well. Being a trained milliner also granted Bev the added skill of not only designing and creating stunning original garments, but matching hats as well.

Some years later she decided that instead of sewing for everyone else, she would like to teach and show others how to create their own garments. Bev attended many training courses and eventually she was accepted to teach at Queensland's Technical Education Colleges. Over the years she taught bridal headwear, lingerie, swimwear, and surface embellishment courses at these colleges. She delights in being able to show eager students what can be achieved with fabric, thread, and a domestic sewing machine.

In 1990 Brisbane held its inaugural 'Stitches and Craft Show', and it was with great delight that Bev began demonstrating machine embroidery in the public arena. Up to that stage she had not ventured much into embroidery and so it presented her with a huge challenge. After much practice, however, Bev perfected her techniques for what she now likes to call 'free-stitching' machine embroidery.

Bev is a walking advertisement for what she does. Admiring glances and compliments about her embroidered garments have led to much interest in her exquisite stitching, and invitations to teach her 'free-stitching' machine embroidery at the colleges, as well as sewing machine and fabric stores around Australia.

Bev's favorite aspect of her chosen textile art is being able to bring embroidery to the point where the stitches appear life-like. This makes her feel that she is fulfilling her goals and dreams. Bev loves her embroidery designs to tell a story, and takes much of her inspiration from flowers and such Australian characters as Blinky Bill, the koala with his tartan waistcoat and bushman's hat.

As a result of her expertise and knowledge, Bev was invited to set the exhibitors' criteria for free-motion embroidery in the Fine Arts category of the Queensland Royal National Show (which is held annually), and she has been a judge every year since then.

Bev's work is so exquisitely precise and amazingly accurate, it denies the fact that it is all hand-guided free-motion machine embroidery. Her machine embroidery can aptly be defined as 'fine art', with the machine needle as her brush, the thread her paint, and Bev herself the master artist.

Email Bev (bev@freestitching.com) or visit her website (www.freestitching.com) for information on her classes.

# ABSTRACT EIGHT
## *Bev Unwin*

Bev's canvas is white linen, with the chrysanthemums created with free-stitched machine embroidery. As one of the challenge elements, the number '8' had to be incorporated into the work, and so Bev reduced the size of the '8' and then cut it out of metal mesh, folding it to represent a butterfly. When you look at the butterfly, the shadow completes the other set of butterfly wings – very clever!

HETTY VAN BOVEN
ESK, QLD, AUSTRALIA

# hetty van boven

Hetty's introduction to patchwork and quilting was through American magazines and books in the early 1980s. She taught herself the basics and by 1984 she was passing on her knowledge and skills locally in the Brisbane Valley, about sixty miles (one hundred kilometers) west of Brisbane.

WHEN THE QUEENSLAND QUILTERS was founded, Hetty wrote some articles for their newsletter and was soon invited to teach for them in Brisbane.

With her passion for the craft, her own skills were constantly improving through books, magazines, and workshops with Australian and overseas tutors. She became a very busy and popular tutor who kept developing new and interesting classes for the many groups that invited her back on a regular basis.

Teaching classes took her all over Queensland, as well as interstate, Canada, the US, the Netherlands, and Norfolk Island. She was invited to teach online at www.quiltuniversity. com, where she taught *Fabric Postcards* from 2005 to 2007. At the same time she conducted 'Quilt ESKapes', her twice-yearly quilting retreat that ran from 1994 to 2008 and catered for isolated quilting enthusiasts.

A love of writing saw Hetty's projects published in such popular Australian magazines as *Down Under Quilts* (the first Aussie quilting magazine), *Australian Patchwork & Quilting*, *Quilters' Companion* and *Australian Country Craft*. Other publications include From *Australia with Love ... A Patchwork Year* (published in 1990 by Yvonne Rein and Kathie Nutt, the founders of *Down Under Quilts*), and *From My Garden, with Love: An Elegant Quilt in Shadow Appliqué* (self-published in 1997). In 2003 Martingale in the US published *Hetty's Shadow Appliqué: A Fresh Take on a Traditional Technique*.

In the late 1980s Hetty began teaching the *Double Wedding Ring* quilt. Being way ahead of her time and realizing a need for acrylic templates, she developed a kit with templates and an instruction booklet.

Hetty went on to tutor many *Double Wedding Ring* workshops and continued to fine-tune the instructions. The templates gradually improved and in 2006 she collaborated with Victorian Textiles to sell the booklet with their fantastic templates.

Hetty's work has been exhibited extensively in Australia as well as in the US, Canada, and the Netherlands. One of her many highlights has been the 'Obsessions' exhibition held at Toowoomba in Queensland in 2008, in collaboration with her daughter-in-law Sharon and well-known longarm quilter Kathy Adams.

Having been interested in the Tarot for decades, Hetty has finally created twenty-two textile works based on the Major Arcana, using a diverse range of techniques, fabrics, threads, and embellishments with an organic, intuitive process. It is only now, at this time in her career, that Hetty has the skills, fabric stash, and time to create such amazing masterpieces.

After twenty-five years of designing projects for classes, books, and magazines, Hetty is now thoroughly relishing her retirement with husband Gerry and making quilts for her family; and she finally has the time to go to those art classes she never had time for before.

Hetty's CV reads like a book and she is too modest to mention all her achievements. Suffice it to say she is a master artisan and an Australian quilting icon.

**You can contact Hetty via email (hetty@westnet.com.au). Even though she has retired she would love to hear from you!**

# BERNINA BLING
## *Hetty van Boven*

*Bernina Bling* was created in the same style Hetty used in her *'Obsessions'* exhibition – interesting fabrics such as velvet, silk, and jacquards, with opulent amounts of machine embellishment, and adorned with beading and silver curios. Being able to bring them all together on her much loved Bernina *1230* allows her to express her bliss in using such a vast array of materials and techniques.

MARIYA WATERS
DONCASTER, VIC., AUSTRALIA

Mariya Waters is an international and Australian award-winning quiltmaker and teacher. She has been married to her husband Gavin for thirty-five years and has two children – Elizabeth and Alan. As a New Zealand expatriate wife, Mariya began quilting in New Zealand in 1989 and was juried into the first New Zealand National Quilt Competition with her first quilt. In 1994, while living in England, her third quilt won the prestigious Ascot Trophy at the National Quilt Association competition.

SINCE THEN MARIYA HAS SPECIALIZED in designing and making quilts for exhibition. All the exhibition quilts she has completed since 1994 have won both local and international awards. Many of her quilts have appeared in magazines, books, and advertisements, and her quilts have been acquired for public and private collections. Although she currently specializes in hand appliqué with machine quilting and trapunto in both large and miniature formats, Mariya has also won international awards for a series of innovative pieced quilts.

In 1999 Mariya moved from England to Melbourne, Australia where she became an accredited state quilt appraiser. Mariya continues to teach her classes in hand appliqué, machine quilting, and trapunto, which are in high demand.

After working for about 17,000 hours (that's almost four years full-time) on her latest masterwork quilt, *Renaissance Revival*, the quilt was awarded the 2007 'Best of Australia'

award, the prestigious 'Founders' award at the International Quilt Association Market and Festival held in Houston, Texas. Then in April 2009 Mariya's Renaissance Revival quilt was awarded Best of Show in the American Quilters' Society Quilt Contest – an acquisition contest in Paduca, Kentucky. Renaissance Revival is now in the permanent collection at the National Quilt Museum of the USA. Mariya's latest miniature, Blue Birds in Paradise, won second place at the IQA Market and Festival, third in the American Quilters' Show in Paduca, and has since been purchased for private collection.

Mariya's philosophy on quilting is: 'If it can be drawn it can be constructed – somehow!'

**You can contact Mariya via email (mariya.waters@yahoo.com.au) or visit her website (www.mariyawaters.com) to view her quilts and teaching schedule.**

mariya waters

# LET'S CELEBR8
## *Mariya Waters*

Mariya's challenge is a cut-work 'celebr8ory' announcement card with a lined baronial envelope, featuring the graphic '8' in an illuminated letter style. The card has been constructed over a heavy stabilizer using cut-work and satin stitch appliqué, and incorporating three-dimensional applied elements. Machine embroidered with polyester and silver thread, it is decorated with Swarovski crystals.
*Cre8, decor8, illumin8, celebr8*

CAROL WILKES
MALENY, QLD, AUSTRALIA

Being a well-recognized textile artist and tutor, Carol uses fabrics, threads, and mixed media as her artistic language.

Carol is an experienced, multi-skilled textile artist and tutor who refers to herself as a 'surface embellishment technician' – she is an experimentalist in both embroidery and contemporary quiltmaking, along with fashion design techniques.

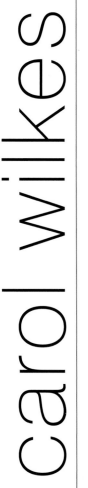

carol wilkes

HER CREATIVE ARTISTRY, free-motion embroidery, and collage techniques have developed as a result of her passion for fabric and trends. Combining both traditional and current practices, she renders textile surfaces with her own uniquely individual style.

Carol's background is that of a hand embroiderer, quiltmaker, and tutor.

Exposure to free-motion embroidery sparked her transition from traditional embroidery practices into the world of contemporary textiles.

Her textile artworks are identified by her use of fabric, threads, mixed media, and free-motion embroidery, which she combines with contemporary practices to create finished artworks, contemporary wall quilts, and fashion items. Carol's creative artistry, embroidery, and collage techniques have resulted from a passion for fabric and fashion, and her relentless desire to deconstruct and reconstruct.

The sewing machine is an important extension of Carol's obsession – after all it is her ultimate art-tool. Carol and her Bernina have become one as she illustrates her ideas in stitch, ultimately developing her artistic voice. Carol spends endless hours playing with a technique, and the same amount of time sampling and experimenting with some of the more interesting outcomes (which in turn create even more possibilities for her to play with). The process is infinite.

Carol has had her work displayed in group exhibitions between 1996 and 2007, both in Australia and internationally.

She is renowned for her teaching, workshop, and tutoring skills, and has been invited to share her vast knowledge at forums and educational institutes throughout Australia (where she has run master classes for the past few years), New Zealand, and Japan.

Carol's artistic career has been supported by such grants and awards as The NSW Quilters' Guild Inc. sponsorship program 2000, the ADF 2007 Grant from Caloundra City Council (on the east coast of Australia), along with many others between 1999 and 2007 throughout Australia.

Carol has been featured in many Australian publications such as *Australia Dreaming Quilts to Nagoya* (published in 1996), *Australian Bounty*, and *Under the Southern Cross*. She has also had her work published in such magazines as *Quilts Japan* (1997), *Down Under Quilts* (1996-97), *Craft Arts International* (1995-96), and numerous textile-related publications. She has been a guest judge, lecturer, and she wrote critiques at various forums throughout her career, as well as textile and fashion awards.

Her textile works of art are represented in collections worldwide, including in Japan, New Zealand, England, and the USA.

**You can contact Carol via email (carolwilkes@malenynet.com) for more information on her appearances and class schedules.**

# RED TAPE
## *Carol Wilkes*

Carol realized that there were to be hours and hours of work ahead of her, and so her technique of choice for *Red Tape* was the free-machine embroidered cord. The foundation fabric was constructed using small fragments of leftover fabric – this collection of 'bits' was then turned into a collage on tulle to create a foundation fabric.

Carol's personal criteria would be to present a contemporary art-to-wear garment that had a visual impact, tone, and texture, predominantly using a single technique and its many variables. Most importantly, her garment had to give maximum indulgence, pleasure, and curiosity to both the viewer and the wearer. Blending, fusing, layering, coiling, and realizing the numerous spontaneous alternatives, her obsessive nature and curiosity for variation led her to create and combine various assemblage ideas for the textured cloth to create her garment titled *Red Tape*. Cords were used to create fabric, wispy edges, and ends for additional texture and sculptural effects as well as to embellish the fabric surface. Carol's creations are designed from a traditional pattern that seemed to take on a life of its own, becoming fabric wraps to drape and adorn the body. Both the hat and bag featured cords, crinoline, red tape, wispy edges, and foam balls covered in fabric. The unlined bag, though totally non-functional, is meant only as a thing of beauty.

WENDY WRIGHT, ADVA/TEXTILES
TOOWOOMBA, QLD, AUSTRALIA

# wendy wright

Wendy's garments are not produced lightly or flippantly but evolve through an interpretation of her surroundings as seen through her eyes. Traveling to different teaching locations throughout Australia has given Wendy the opportunity to absorb the magnificent Australian landscape. Images are encapsulated in a subliminal way, and then lie in wait until an illusive magic moment triggers that image. A theme then keeps 'hassling' Wendy, wanting to be developed, and the original idea then becomes linked to a design, color and texture. Each piece is created in her head many times as she turns it inside out, overcoming problems, and then chooses techniques to suit. When this 'percolating' process is complete, Wendy becomes a slave, dedicated to this new creation until it is completed.

FABRICS AND THREADS ARE DYED, designs fine-tuned, and beads selected, with Wendy working along with each piece, 'listening' to it, always at the ready, to go with little changes here and there as they present themselves. Sometimes there are happy accidents which teach her new techniques and offer new creative opportunities.

Hundreds of hours later, when the dream in Wendy's head has become a reality, she experiences a feeling of elation. Only then can she walk away from her creation. The construction of her 'head picture' has been a journey of creativity, a release of emotions, and a great sense of satisfaction.

Wendy's textile art career started in 1975 with training by leading sewing machine companies. In 1985 she then received her Teaching Certificate and went on to achieve an Associate Diploma of Visual Arts/Textiles in 1988, which led her to the E'Col de Haute Couture – pattern, flower making, and millinery – in 1993.

In 2009, Wendy's work was acquired by the Queensland Museum for their contemporary collection. Before that, in 2001-02, she was Finalist and Winner of the Judges' Award at the 'International Fairfield Fashion Awards' in the USA, which toured the US and Europe. She also took out the Major Prize of the 'Sulky of America Thread Competition', as well as being Finalist in the Powerhouse Museum's 'International Lace Exhibition'.

In the 1990s Wendy exhibited at the Marriott Hotel in Brisbane; in the 'Art to Wear' exhibition held in conjunction with the Quilt and Craft Fair at Darling Harbour in Sydney; was a Finalist and Major Prize Winner of the 'Wearable Wool Awards' in Armidale, New South Wales; and she was Finalist for several years as well as overall Design Award Winner (1996) in the NZ 'Wearable Art Awards'.

Since 1980 Wendy has been involved in solo and group exhibitions throughout Australia and overseas, with her work being acquired by private collectors.

Wendy is a much sought after tutor, teacher, and demonstrator, as well as a well recognized and highly acclaimed textile artist in the art-to-wear world. Her creative works are identified by their lace-filament-like appearance, and noted for their stylish cut and design.

**You can contact Wendy via email (wendywright@bigpond.com) for information on her garments and classes.**

# THE ULTIMATE SHRUG
*Wendy Wright, ADVA/Textiles*

*The Ultimate Shrug* was made with layers of black, white, and red fantasy yarn trailed onto water-soluble backing and then stitched with black, white, and silver metallic threads through a single needle, to hold the yarn together to create a fabric. The 8s are incorporated into the lace-like fabric and appear as stripes and a feature border on the shrug, representing how Bernina is an integral part of all Wendy's creations. The shrug pattern is original and multi-sized.

# Jenny Haskins DESIGNS
## ... for elegant embroidery

# JENNY HASKINS' DESIGN COLLECTION

*Jenny's inspirational design catalog, for when you plan your next embroidered quilt.*

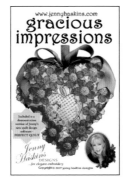

lottie's poppies
www.jennyhaskins.com

robyn's romance
www.jennyhaskins.com

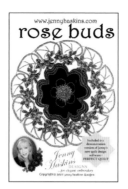
rose buds
www.jennyhaskins.com

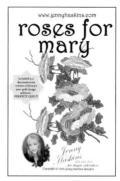
roses for mary
www.jennyhaskins.com

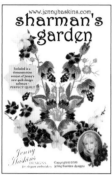
sharman's garden
www.jennyhaskins.com

simon's terrific trims
www.jennyhaskins.com

twin needle shadow work by machine
www.jennyhaskins.com

victorian bows & baskets
www.jennyhaskins.com

victorian embroidery the heart
www.jennyhaskins.com

victorian fantasy with fans
www.jennyhaskins.com

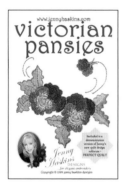
victorian pansies
www.jennyhaskins.com

victorian piano shawl
www.jennyhaskins.com

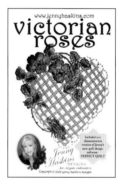
victorian roses
www.jennyhaskins.com

victorian script & antique frames
www.jennyhaskins.com

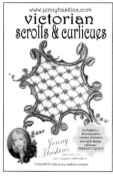
victorian scrolls & curlicues
www.jennyhaskins.com

vintage needlework
www.jennyhaskins.com

*Remember, the more you share your love of machine artistry and quilting the more there is to share, and you will be amazed where it will lead you. So get busy sharing! In the meantime, Jenny and Simon are busy planning their next quilt and book (When Dreams Flower) – one that will continue to bring joy to the creative eye and soul in every one of us.*

## Available from:

Unique Creative Opportunities (Australia), or email for the contact details of US distributors of all Jenny's and Simon's products, threads, and stabilizers.

Phone: 61 2 9680 1381

Fax: 61 2 9680 1381

Email: simon@jennyhaskins.com

Web: www.jennyhaskins.com

# OTHER BOOKS/MAGAZINES BY JENNY HASKINS

| | |
|---|---|
| Victorian Dreams | Sally Milner Publications |
| Color Purple | (sold out) See *Creative Expressions* No 12 & No 13 for directions |
| The Federation Quilt | (sold out) See *Creative Expressions* No 15 to send for directions on a similar quilt |
| Amadeus | Aussie Publishing (sold out) |
| Inspirational Machine Embroidered Quilting (Arsenic and Old Lace quilt) | Aussie Publishing (sold out) |
| Victorian Pansies | Quilter's Resource (sold out) |
| Victorian Roses | Quilter's Resource (sold out) |
| Victorian Splendor | Quilter's Resource (sold out) |
| Inspirational Home Décor | Brother Australia (sold out) |
| Latte Quilt with Kerrie Hay | Quilter's Resource |
| Roses for Mary | Quilter's Resource and Unique Creative |
| MarJen for Error, *CE Special* | Pride Publishing (Creative Living Media) |
| Simon's Folly, *CE Special* | Pride Publishing (Creative Living Media) |
| Spectacular Fashion, *CE Special* | Pride Publishing (Creative Living Media) |
| Moulin Rouge, *CE Special* | Pride Publishing (Creative Living Media) |
| Fragrant Delights, *CE Special* | Creative Living Media |
| *Creative Expressions* Magazine | Creative Living Media |
| Aquamarine Ambience | Quilter's Resource and Unique Creative |
| Summer Wine | Quilter's Resource and Unique Creative |
| Jenny's Heritage | RNK Distributing and Unique Creative |
| Sharman's Vintage Garden | RNK Distributing and Unique Creative |
| A Galleria of Machine Artistry and Quilting | Brewers Quilting and Sewing Supplies and Unique Creative |